# JourneyThrough®

# Haggai & Malachi

30 Biblical Insights by **Michael Wittmer**

*Journey Through Haggai & Malachi*
© 2019 by Michael Wittmer
Published by Discovery House Publishing Singapore Pte. Ltd.
All rights reserved.

Discovery House Publishing™ is affiliated
with Our Daily Bread Ministries Asia Ltd.

Requests for permission to quote
from this book should be directed to:

Permissions Department
Our Daily Bread Publishing
P. O. Box 3566
Grand Rapids, MI 49501, USA

Or contact us by email at
permissionsdept@odb.org



Cover design by Joshua Tan
Typeset by Lidya Jap

ISBN 978-981-49-9128-5

# Foreword

Are you stuck in a rut? You started something—a job, friendship, or perhaps marriage—that you've lost the heart to finish. You began with high hopes, but the reality is falling short of your dreams. This is not what you signed up for. Problem is, you're in too far to quit. You can't back out, and you can't go on. *What to do?*

Read Haggai and Malachi! These prophets speak to us from the discouragement of Scripture's middle. The Old Testament is ending, and the story isn't going well. Israel, God's chosen people, had returned from exile, excited to rebuild their temple. But when they laid the foundation, they saw it would never measure up to the former temple built by King Solomon (see 1 Kings 7:13–51, Ezra 3:12). They lost heart. And when their neighbours intimidated them, they quit.

Haggai enters. He inspires them to get up and go on. They finish the temple, but it isn't as glorious as the first. Their discouragement breeds cynicism that smothers their devotion to God. *What's the point? Our best days are behind us.* Malachi appears and urges them forward. Yes, you're stuck, but you're stuck in the middle of something that God loves. The first half is over, and it was disappointing. The second half belongs to God, so keep moving!

May these prophets encourage you to trust God with your disappointments. You can go onward, with hope and joy.

**Mike Wittmer**

## We're glad you've decided to join us on a journey into a deeper relationship with Jesus Christ!

The *Journey Through* series is designed to help believers spend time with God in His Word, book by book. Each title is written by a faithful Bible teacher to help you read, reflect, and apply God's Word, a little bit at a time. It's a great accompaniment to be read alongside the Bible, as you dig deeper into God's Word. We trust the meditation on God's Word will draw you into a closer relationship with Him through our Lord and Saviour, Jesus Christ.

## How to use this resource

READ: After reading and reflecting on the Bible verses, use the explanatory notes to help you understand the Scriptures in fresh ways.

REFLECT: Use the questions to consider how you could respond to God and His Word, letting Him change you from the inside out.

RECORD: Jot down your thoughts and responses in the space provided to keep a diary of your journey with the Lord.

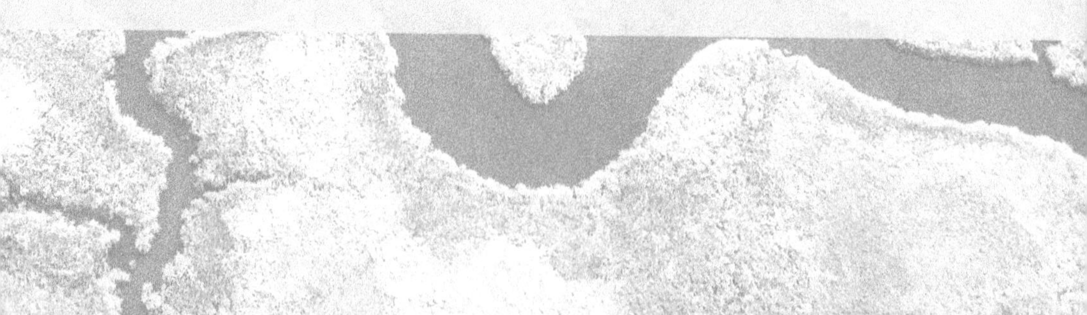

# An Overview

Haggai appears in 520 BC, nearly 20 years after the first Jewish exiles had returned to Jerusalem and begun rebuilding the temple. Haggai teams with Zechariah to encourage the remnant to obey God and finish the job, overcoming both external threats and internal despair. Haggai delivers four prophecies that alternate between God's commands and promises.

| | |
|---|---|
| 1:1–15 | *Command:* Build the temple for blessing |
| 2:1–9 | *Promise:* This temple will be glorious |
| 2:10–19 | *Command:* Build the temple for holiness and blessing |
| 2:20–23 | *Promise:* David's Messianic line will be established |

Malachi prophesies about 80 years later, most likely between 450 and 430 BC. He is a contemporary of Ezra and Nehemiah, and with them urges Judah to return to their covenant relationship with God. The finished temple did not deliver the glory that Haggai had promised, and the disillusioned nation doubted God's love and offered half-hearted, cynical worship.

Malachi asks a series of questions that exposes their unfaithfulness, assures them of God's love, and calls them to renew their covenant with God.

Introduction (1:1)
    A.   First Disputation: *God's covenantal love in election* (1:2–5)
        B.   Second Disputation: *Breaking covenant through blemished sacrifices* (1:6–2:9)
            C.   Third Disputation: *Breaking covenant through divorce* (2:10–16)
            C¹.  Fourth Disputation: *Breaking covenant through injustice* (2:17–3:5)
        B¹.  Fifth Disputation: *Breaking covenant by withholding tithes* (3:6–12)
    A¹.  Sixth Disputation: *God's covenantal love in judgment* (3:13–4:3)
Conclusion (4:4–6)

# Day 1

**Read** Haggai 1:1–4

Have you ever walked into the middle of a story? You come upon two friends who are arguing. You want to help, but don't know how until you listen for a while. You need to learn the backstory—who did what that led to the dispute.

The first thing we notice about Haggai is we are walking into the middle of a story. The prophet received God's word during the second year of King Darius, and he delivered the message to Zerubbabel the governor and Joshua the high priest (Haggai 1:1). Who are these people? We learn their backstory in Ezra 1–6. A Persian king had permitted God's people to return to Jerusalem and rebuild the temple. They laid the foundation, then stopped for 20 years when their neighbours opposed them. They realised their temple wasn't going to be as magnificent as Solomon's anyway (see 1 Kings 6). They figured they might as well stay home and remodel their own houses.

The second thing we notice about Haggai is we're walking into the middle of an argument. The people say, "The time has not yet come to rebuild the Lord's house." The "Lord Almighty" replies, and He is not happy (Haggai 1:2–4). The name "Lord Almighty" occurs 14 times in Haggai and 55 times in Malachi. It means "Yahweh of Armies" and underscores God's invincible rule.

What would you expect the most powerful being in the universe to say? Something glorious? Something victorious? Here's a wonderful truth about our God. **He doesn't use His strength to squash us, but stoops to our level and looks us in the eye.** He asks, "Is it a time for you yourselves to be living in your panelled houses, while this house remains a ruin?" (v. 4).

God mentions time because "time" was His children's excuse. They wouldn't concede that they had given up on the dream of rebuilding the Lord's temple. They argued that it was still there, it just wasn't the right time. And it hadn't been for 20 years! Discouraged people make excuses, then distract themselves with lesser things.

God realises His children are stalled by fear and failure. The future feels closed, so God opens up possibilities with a question. That's the magic of questions. They're open-ended; they invite us to imagine what might seem impossible. Questions perk up our ears, set our wheels turning, and get us dreaming again.

Where do you feel stuck? It may be a marriage, or perhaps a child who

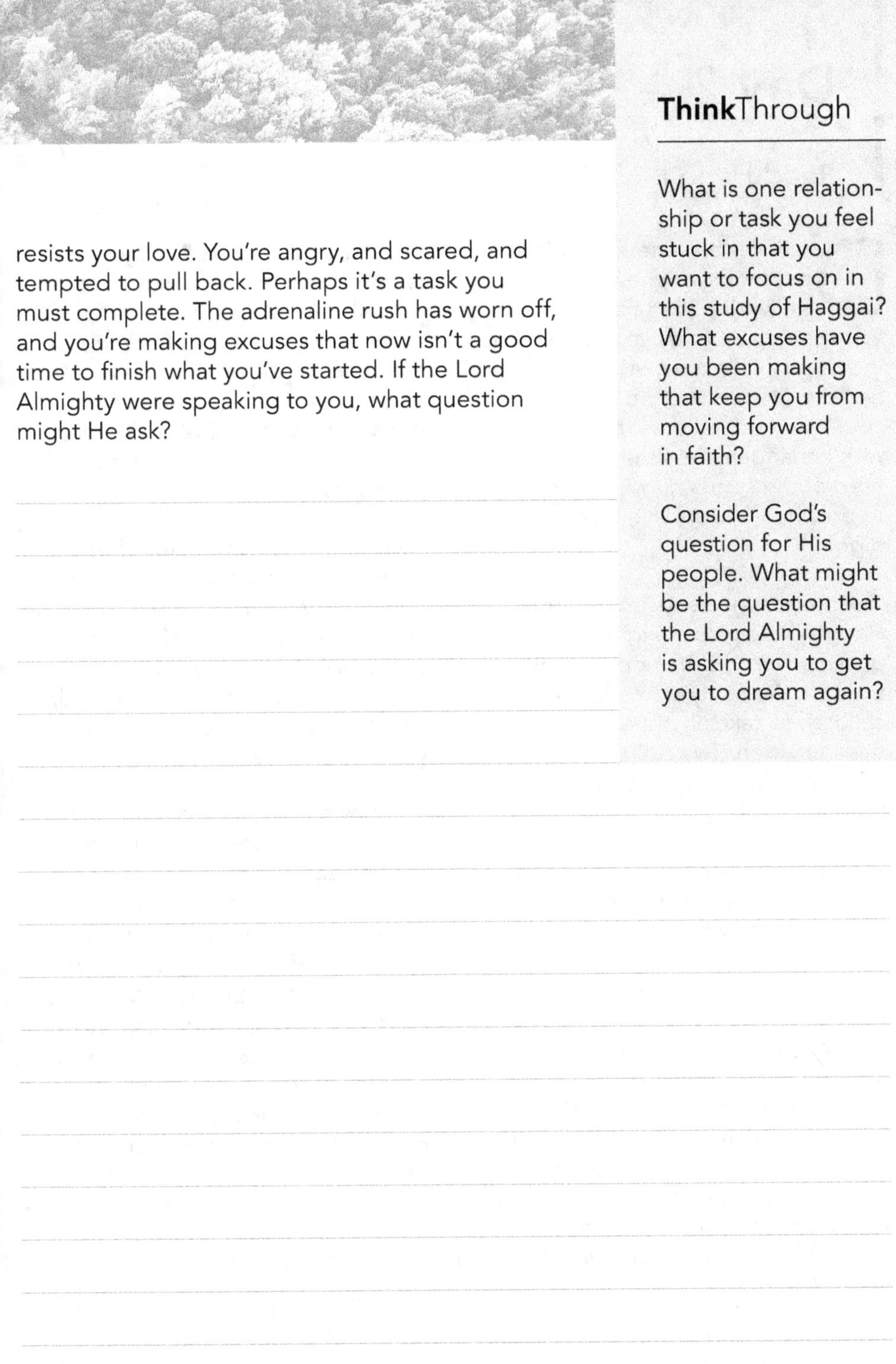

resists your love. You're angry, and scared, and tempted to pull back. Perhaps it's a task you must complete. The adrenaline rush has worn off, and you're making excuses that now isn't a good time to finish what you've started. If the Lord Almighty were speaking to you, what question might He ask?

# **Day** 2



Dr. Phil is an American celebrity psychologist known for delivering hard truths candidly. When he encounters someone mired in self-pity or in a rut of poor choices, he asks, "How's that working for you?" He understands that people won't change unless they're sick and tired of the status quo. The first thing to do when you are in a hole is stop digging!

God makes the same point through Haggai. After providing a glimmer of hope with His previous question, the Lord Almighty now urges His children to take an honest look at their situation. Twice, God says, "Give careful thought to your ways" (Haggai 1:5, 7).

The first time when God tells them to consider their ways, He wants them to acknowledge how futile their stalled lives have become. They work hard but have little to show for their efforts. They eat but are never full; layer on clothes but are never warm; and seem to put their money "in a purse with holes in it" (v. 6). *What's the use of all their labour?* Are you fed up with your current situation? Only after we recognise the futility of our ways can we move on to God's second "Give careful thought to your ways" (v. 7).

This time the Lord Almighty invites Israel to consider why they're stuck. He tells them that He had blown away the fruit of their labour because they had forgotten Him. He was disciplining them because of His house "which remains a ruin, while each of you is busy with your own house" (v. 9).

You and I may not be stuck because of our Father's discipline, but if we feel stuck it's at least in part because we've taken our eyes off Him. It's impossible to feel stuck for long when we're living for our true end, "which is Christ in you, the hope of glory" (Colossians 1:27).

We may feel mired in a relationship or project that seems mundane. It doesn't seem to be working, and even if it did, it wouldn't be great. *What's the use of labouring?* **To get out of the rut, we need to confess that we are stuck and cry out to God for help.** Our circumstances may not change immediately, but our perspective will. We will view our situation from God's perspective, and that will make all the difference.

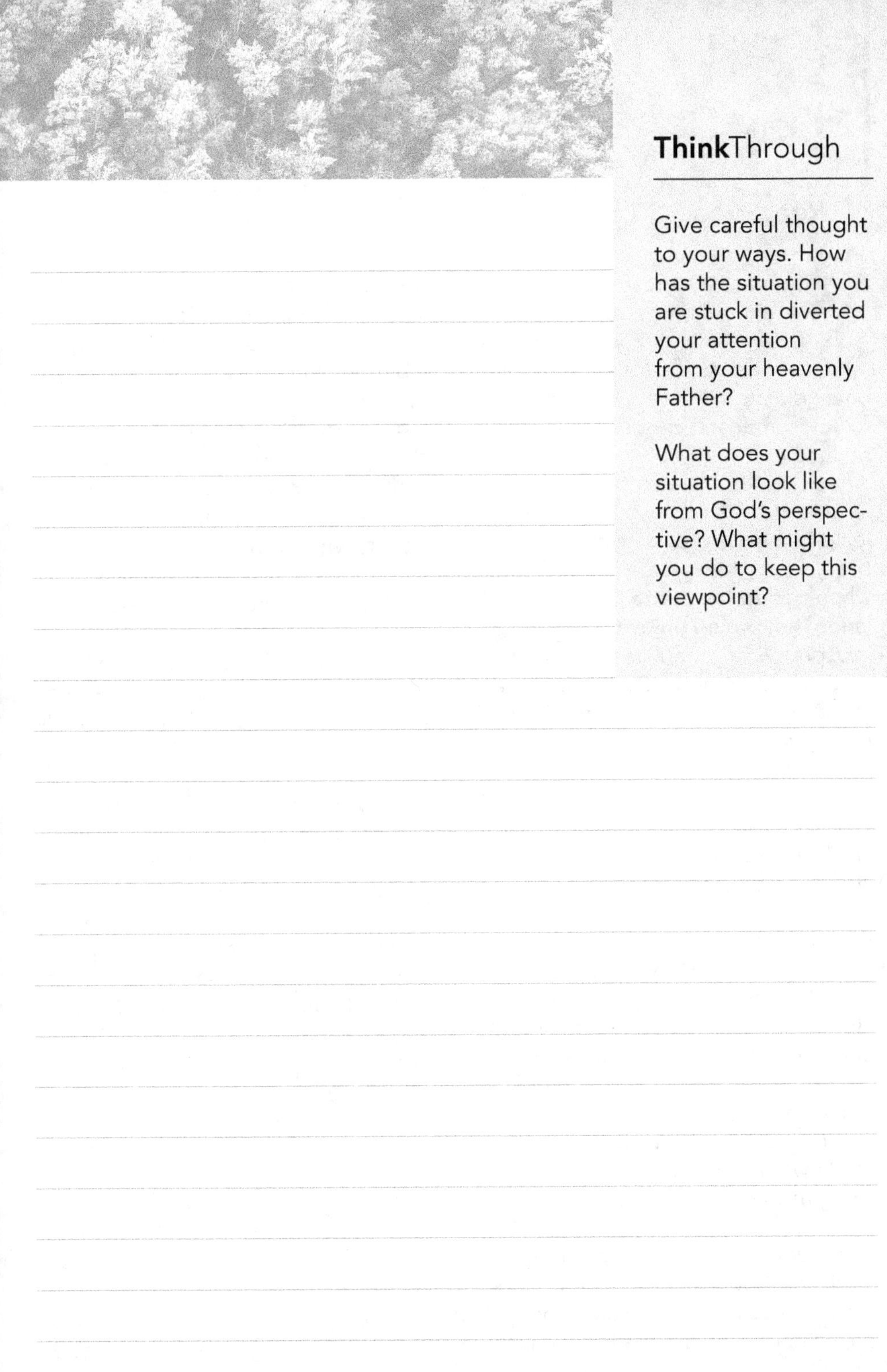


ThinkThrough

Give careful thought to your ways. How has the situation you are stuck in diverted your attention from your heavenly Father?

What does your situation look like from God's perspective? What might you do to keep this viewpoint?

# Day 3

**Read** Haggai 1:5–11

You may have heard people say we should never act out of fear. They're wrong. If you're jogging in the woods and hear the growl of a bear you shouldn't say, "I choose not to act from fear. I choose love." You'll be lunch!

God leads with hope, but He doesn't leave out an appropriate fear. He promised to bless Israel's obedience when He led them into the promised land. They would enjoy peace and prosperity, large families and bumper crops (Deuteronomy 28:1–14). In that same breath, He also warned them of the consequences for disobedience (vv. 15–68).

At the entrance to the promised land, God warned Israel that disobedience would heap upon their heads the curses of the covenant. Everything that should have gone right would go painfully wrong. They would suffer loss after loss until they returned to Him (vv. 15–68). Israel rejected God anyway and was exiled into Babylon. God knows that He is our life, and that disregarding Him will inevitably ruin our lives. He loves us too much to allow that, so He disciplines us to bring us back to himself.

Now Judah is back in the promised land, but they still haven't learned their lesson. They're stuck because they haven't put God and His temple first.

So God disciplines them again, calling for "a drought on the fields . . . on people and livestock, and on all the labour of your hands" (Haggai 1:11).

God loves us too much not to discipline us. **Whether or not our suffering is for any specific sin, every trial seeks to turn our hearts towards Him.** God tells us to "endure hardship as discipline" (Hebrews 12:7), knowing that our Father only "disciplines the [ones] he loves" (v. 6). It's no fun being stuck, but our predicament does force our eyes to look above and lock firmly onto God.

The Lord Almighty must be our number one pursuit, whether we feel like we're winning, stuck in a rut, or just starting out. For the children of Israel, pursuing God meant going up into the mountains and bringing down timber to "build [God's] house, so that [God] may take pleasure in it and be honoured" (Haggai 1:8). What does pursuing God mean for you today?

ThinkThrough

How might God be
using fear to lead
you back to follow-
ing Him?

What were some
ways you pursued
God in the past?
What might pursuing
God look like for you
in this season of life?

# Day 4



Moby Dick narrates Captain Ahab's obsessive pursuit of a great white whale. First mate Starbuck understood the risk, saying, "I will have no man in my boat who isn't afraid of a whale." He knew that "an utterly fearless man [was] a far more dangerous comrade than a coward". A sailor who isn't afraid might become careless and put the whole boat in danger.

Perhaps you've grappled with your stuck situation by telling yourself that in the big scheme of things, it's not that important. It's just one relationship, one job, one missed opportunity. Life goes on. This may be true, and helpful to remember. Your fear may have lifted as you put it in this perspective. But if we're not careful, our lack of fear could make us careless. We might become sloppy and put others at risk. We might not fear our situation, but there is something we must fear.

The situation in Jerusalem seemed insignificant. A small band of settlers were staring at a half-finished temple. Haggai calls them "the whole remnant" (Haggai 1:12), which sounds pathetic, like "large fragment" or "leftovers". The stakes seemed small. So what if their temple remained unfinished?

Their little project mattered because God said it mattered. He commanded them to get up and get moving, and the bedraggled group obeyed because they "feared the LORD" (v. 12). They weren't impressed with their assignment; they were impressed with the One who gave it. That made all the difference.

How do we learn to fear the Lord? By remembering who He is and what He has done. Israel was commanded to regularly assemble to hear the Scriptures, "so that they can listen and learn to fear the LORD" (Deuteronomy 31:11–12). We learn to fear the Lord by reading the Bible and gathering with God's people to worship Him and hear His Word. **The more we know the Lord, the more we would fear Him.**

How can we tell whether we fear the Lord? Simple. Are we doing what He says? The remnant obeyed the Lord because they feared Him. If obedience rises from fearing the Lord, then obedience is the surest way to know we do.

Here's the best part. When the people feared the Lord, He "stirred up . . . the spirit of the whole remnant" (Haggai 1:14). We aren't responsible to motivate ourselves, supply our own pep talk, or marinate ourselves in positive thoughts. We only need to look up from our muddle and fear the Lord. He will stir our hearts.



Do you have a "little project" from God that doesn't seem like an impressive assignment? How might today's reading encourage you?

What does it mean for you to fear the Lord? Are you fearing the Lord in your current situation?

# Day 5

**Read** Haggai 2:1–5

Often, I discount the words of leaders whose job is to stoke morale. I'm sceptical of the coach who says she still believes in her team after their dismal game. She's probably just trying to make them feel better. And I shrug when the provost says his faculty is the best. He probably said the same thing at his previous school, and he'll likely say the same thing at his next one.

Our God is not like that. He means every word, so we must take all His words seriously. In today's passage, God speaks to Judah "on the twenty-first day of the seventh month" (Haggai 2:1), which means the rejuvenated Jews have been rebuilding the temple for nearly a month. God evaluates their progress, and He doesn't sugar-coat His words. Nearly 70 years have passed since the first temple was destroyed. Few people remain who remember its greatness. Yet God doesn't use Judah's lack of first-hand knowledge to excuse them. He asks, "Who of you is left who saw this house in its former glory? How does it look to you now? Does it not seem to you like nothing?" (v. 3).

God might fail our business leadership courses, but His brutal honesty builds trust. Here is someone you can believe. God tells the unvarnished truth. He means what He says.

We can believe Him when He says "Be strong". He says it three times in Haggai 2:4 because He knows that it's hard to be motivated when your predicament is so bleak. But we can "be strong . . . and work" because the Lord Almighty says, "I am with you" (v. 4).

It wasn't obvious to Judah that God *was* with them. God's glory cloud had filled the temple that Solomon built (1 Kings 8:10–12), but it departed when the Babylonians captured Jerusalem and destroyed the temple (Ezekiel 10). We're not sure the glory cloud ever came back, even after Judah rebuilt the temple. When the Jews looked around, they couldn't always see the Lord was with them. But they could trust His word. God means what He says.

You may not feel that God is with you in your mess. You might think He isn't, because if He is, wouldn't you have seen improvements by now? Do not trust your eyes or your feelings. Believe the one who loves you too much to lie or tell you half-truths. He promises "my Spirit remains among you" (Haggai 2:5). He also says, "Never will I leave you; never will I forsake you" (Hebrews 13:5).

**God may not immediately change our situation, but He**

**promises to be with us. We do not bear our burden alone.** God's presence must not make us complacent—we still need to ask God for progress—but His presence will make us content. God is with you. That's enough. So be strong, and get to work.



Do you feel God is with you? What truth might be a more reliable indicator of God's presence than your feelings?

How is contentment with God's presence the best motivation to work?

# Day 6



Financial advisers tell clients not to check their investment portfolios every day. On any given day, markets may be way up or way down. If they're down, clients may panic sell and lock in their losses. It's much better to remain calm and take the long view. By the time they need their money, their investments should be far ahead from where they are now.

On any given day, the situation you're stuck in might trend downwards. Way downwards. Your plan for digging out is blocked, again. You want to crawl into bed and pull the covers over your head. Entirely understandable. This means you're human, and that you care.

Lift your eyes from your present distress and take the long view. As discouraged as you may feel now, you and your predicament are part of a larger story. God tells Judah, "In a little while I will once more shake the heavens and the earth, the sea and the dry land" (Haggai 2:6). *Once more?* Yes. God is referring to Mount Sinai, which "trembled violently" (Exodus 19:18) when God came down to cut His covenant with Israel and make them His special nation (Haggai 2:5).

God went out with His people from Mount Sinai, inhabiting the tabernacle in the wilderness and then the temple in Jerusalem. That temple was destroyed, and this ragtag remnant is trying to rebuild it. They must not give up, because God promises to deliver. "I will shake all nations, and what is desired by all nations will come, and I will fill this house with glory . . . The glory of this present house will be greater than the glory of the former house" (vv. 7–9).

God's promise points to Jesus, the true temple, God with us, the desire of all nations (John 2:19; Matthew 1:23). God's promise points to the church, the body of Christ and the present temple of God on earth (1 Corinthians 12:12–13; 3:16–17). You are not meant to bear your burden alone. Join a church, where brothers and sisters can help to carry your load. Finally, God's promise points to the new creation, when He will once more shake the heavens and the earth "so that what cannot be shaken may remain" (Hebrews 12:26–27).

It stinks to be stuck, but we can persevere when we remember this won't last forever. **Jesus is returning to fix this planet and restore all things.**

"Therefore, since we are receiving a kingdom that cannot be shaken, let

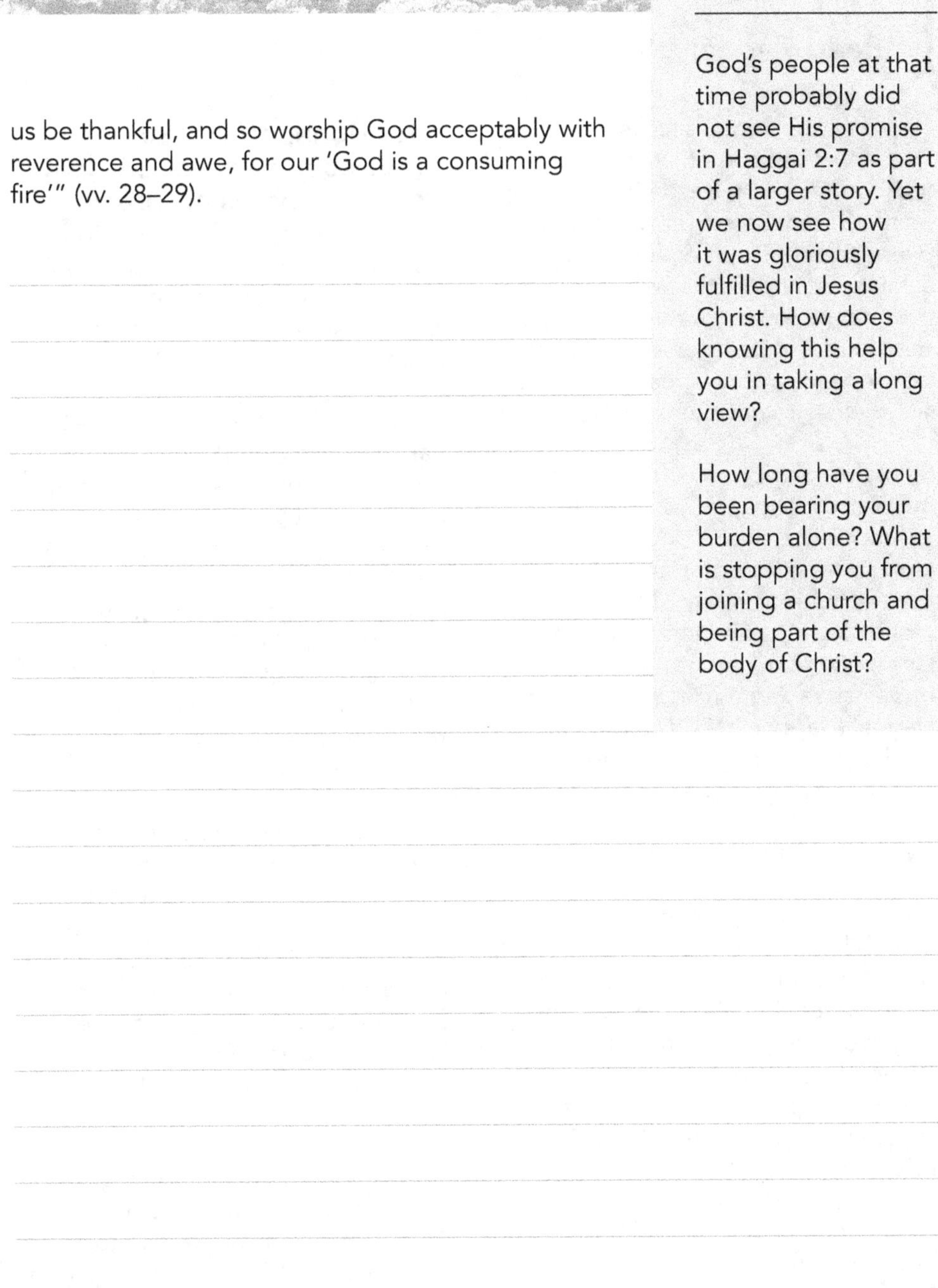

us be thankful, and so worship God acceptably with reverence and awe, for our 'God is a consuming fire'" (vv. 28–29).

# Day 7

**Read** Haggai 2:10–14

Jerry Seinfeld, a successful American comedian, was asked for advice on becoming a comic. Seinfeld said the secret was to write. Every. Single. Day. Seinfeld bought a calendar, and marks an X on every day that he writes jokes. After a few days he has a string of X's. He doesn't worry about writing great jokes; he simply tries to not break the string.

Seinfeld's disciplined effort helps me process today's passage, which at first glance seems oddly off topic. God speaks through Haggai "on the twenty-fourth day of the ninth month", which is 2 months after He last spoke and 4 months since He began speaking through the prophet Haggai (Haggai 2:10). The remnant has been clearing away rubble and rebuilding the temple for a while.

God quizzes the priests on the law. If someone carries consecrated meat in the fold of their garment, the garment itself will become holy (Leviticus 6:27), but what about whatever food the garment touches? Will that become holy too? The priests answered, "No" (Haggai 2:12). What about when an unclean person touches one of these foods? Will it become defiled? The priests said, "Yes" (v. 13).

God's point is that it's easier to become defiled than to be holy. **Holiness requires disciplined, intentional effort. Sin requires nothing at all. Just do what comes naturally.** When we're stuck, we instinctively lash out, plot revenge, or crumple in despair. Who would blame us? That's what most people would do, if left to themselves.

But we're not left to ourselves—God has provided a way! God says this remnant is defiled, so "whatever they do and whatever they offer . . . is defiled" (v. 14). We're not sure why they're defiled—perhaps it's the lingering stench of their idolatry and exile or their failure to rebuild the temple—but either way their solution is the same. Finish the temple. Then they can offer sacrifices that will make them holy.

These animal sacrifices worked because they pointed to Jesus, the perfect lamb of God whose sacrificial death fulfils all sacrifices (Hebrews 9:11–14). Sacrificial lambs could only *cover* sin. Jesus' sacrifice *removes* it. By His "one sacrifice he has made perfect for ever those who are being made holy" (10:14).

Your intractable situation may be worsening by the day. You'd give anything to get out of this mess. Take courage! If you belong to Jesus, the most horrible mire of your life is

resolved. Jesus has set you free from the grip and penalty of sin. You are secure in Him, regardless of what transpires in your situation. You are free in Christ to serve people, even those who contribute to your suffering. Every. Single. Day. Don't break the string.



What is the hardest thing about your intractable situation? How might Jesus free you to tackle this hard thing?

It is human instinct to seek revenge. Does choosing to be holy mean that you will not get justice? How would you explain this to someone seeking revenge?

# Day 8

**Read** Haggai 2:15–19

My friend prays for her wayward son, and she's torn. She wants her son to succeed in life, yet she realises he may not feel his need for Jesus unless he hits rock bottom. So she painfully prays for her son's failure, so that he may come to Jesus and find true success.

Discipline is painful, so it must not be wasted. In a reprise of Haggai 1:5–9, God repeatedly urges the remnant to "give careful thought" to His discipline. He tells them to "give careful thought" to their repeated disappointments. They thought they had "twenty measures" but "there were only ten", "fifty measures" but "there were only twenty" (Haggai 2:15–16). He points to their empty harvests and says, "Give careful thought: Is there yet any seed left in the barn?" (vv. 18–19). There is little fruit, and no seed for planting (v. 19). They're finished!

Why? Because of the people's disobedience. When God made His covenant with Israel, He promised to bless if they obeyed and curse if they disobeyed (see Deuteronomy 28). Israel chose to reject God and disobey. What did they think was going to happen?

God did not establish the same conditions with us, so it's not always clear why God's people suffer today. God may allow us to struggle in our situation to reinforce our reliance on Him, help us avoid complacency, or prevent us from presuming on Him. If He immediately blessed every act of obedience, we might treat God as a cosmic vending machine. We insert our obedience and He plops out His blessing. Perhaps our difficulty is intended to keep us close to God, remembering that our relationship with Him matters more than His reward.

We can't say for sure why God allows us to be stuck, but the purpose is at least in part to turn our hearts towards Him. God tells us to "endure hardship as discipline", for He "is treating you as his children" (Hebrews 12:7). Every father disciplines his children, and refrains from disciplining other people's kids. If we never experience God's firm hand of correction, that's a sign we're not His "true sons and daughters at all" (v. 8).

Thank God for what He's teaching you through your mired muddle. **His discipline is not the goal; it's a necessary path to the goal. God's goal is our growth.** The author of Hebrews admits, "No discipline seems pleasant at the time . . . however, it produces a harvest of righteousness and peace" (v. 11). God's goal is our flourishing. He told Israel their hardship was over. "From

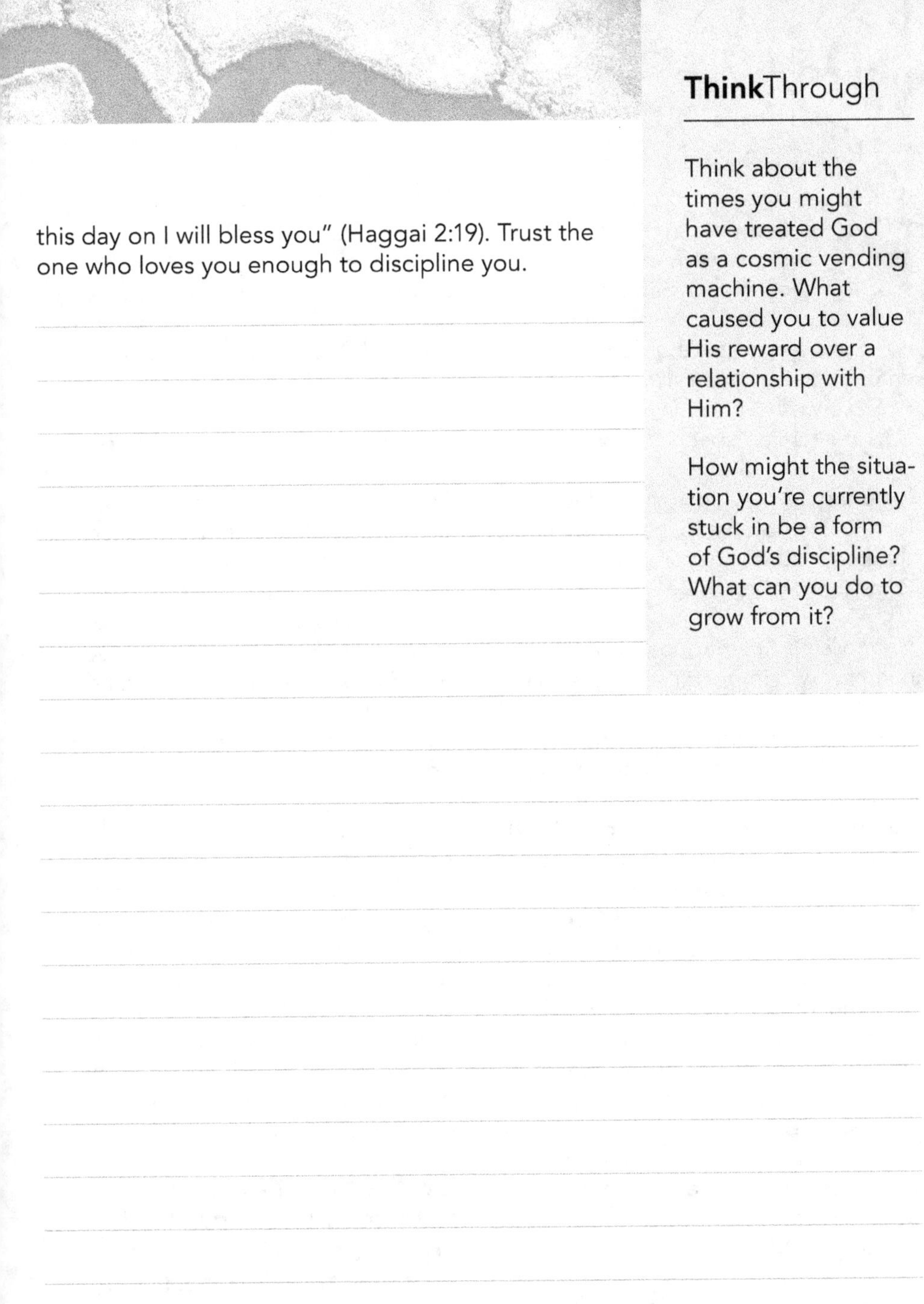

this day on I will bless you" (Haggai 2:19). Trust the one who loves you enough to discipline you.

# Day 9

**Read** Haggai 2:20–22

For the first time in my lifetime, my favourite team made it to the championship game. I was excited, because my team was playing against the defending champion. But I was also nervous, *why did we have to play against the best team?* The coach changed my perspective. He said our team was fortunate to play against the favourite for the championship, because "to be the best you've got to beat the best." Okay then. Let's go!

Haggai's penultimate paragraph contains two important things you've heard before and one thing you haven't. Here's what you've heard before: "Tell Zerubbabel governor of Judah that I am going to shake the heavens and the earth" (Haggai 2:21). This is the fourth time God mentions that Zerubbabel is governor of Judah. Each time may have pained God to say it, and Judah to hear it (1:1, 14; 2:2, 21). Before the exile, Judah had been an independent nation ruled by God through kings. Now it had a governor appointed by the Persian king. Judah was reduced to a tiny, backwater province in someone else's empire. Persian soldiers were stationed nearby, ready to attack at the first sign of trouble. How discouraging!

But God tells Zerubbabel not to despair. As He promised earlier, so He said again that He is "going to shake the heavens and the earth" (v. 21; see v. 6). Don't trust what you see, and definitely don't trust how you feel. God is in charge, and He's gunning for Persia.

How is God going to judge Persia? That's the new information in today's Scriptural reading. God promises to "overturn" and "shatter" enemy forces. He says, "I will overthrow chariots and their drivers; horses and their riders will fall" (v. 22). This was a bold claim. Persia had conquered the world by its unmatched innovations in cavalry and chariots. No army could defeat the Persian warriors on horseback.

Until God. He wanted the world to know that He's better than their very best, so He said, "Great! I'm toppling horses!" And He did. Persia was defeated by the Greeks, who were defeated by the Romans, who were defeated by barbarians, who then settled into various countries of Europe. Empires have come and gone, and look who's still here—the children of Israel!

**God is mightier than your miry situation. He is stronger than its strongest, most distressing part.** Ask Him to defeat your problem at its

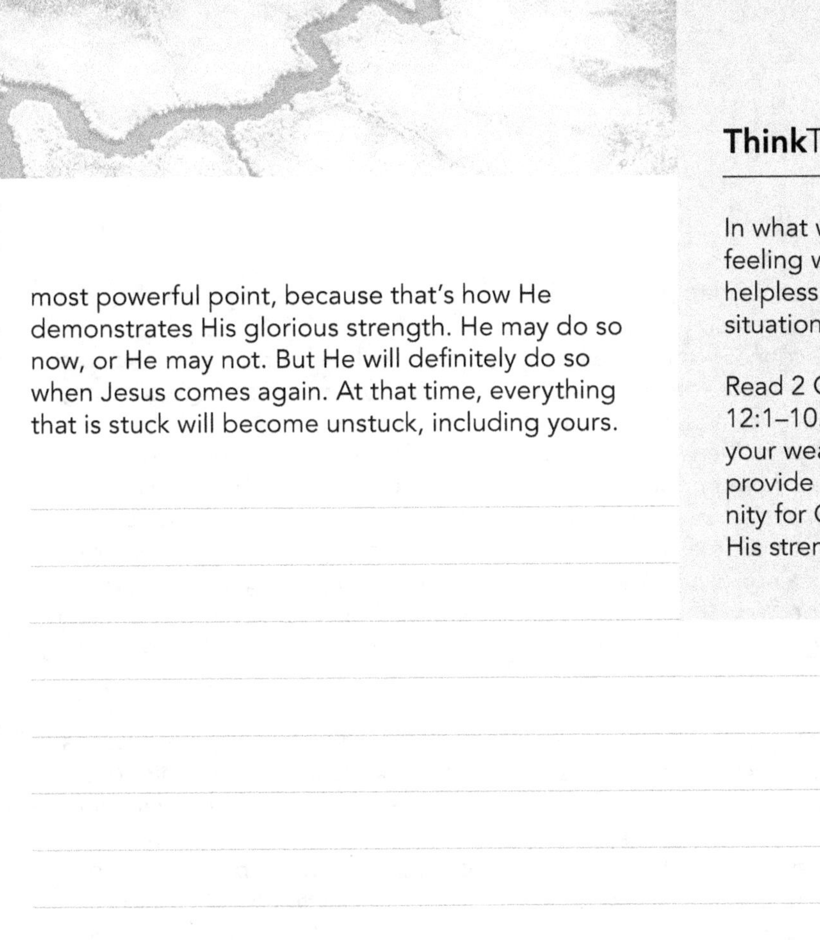

most powerful point, because that's how He demonstrates His glorious strength. He may do so now, or He may not. But He will definitely do so when Jesus comes again. At that time, everything that is stuck will become unstuck, including yours.

# Day 10

**Read** Haggai 2:23

Ponder the meaning of life, and you must inevitably grapple with the connection between you and the cosmos. You seem most important, because it's *you*. But you are not as large as the world, so the world must be more important. The big picture matters more than any one detail. But the details make up the world. If there are no individuals, there would be no world. Ultimately then, a satisfying vision of life must include both you and the world.

And so it does. God concludes the book of Haggai by focusing on the world. "'On that day,' declares the LORD Almighty" (Haggai 2:23). What day is God speaking of? It is the day of the Lord. Several prophets anticipate this climactic day when God's promised Messiah comes to judge and save the world.

This day will *terrify God's enemies*. They will "flee to caves in the rocks and to holes in the ground from the fearful presence of the LORD and the splendour of his majesty, when he rises to shake the earth" (Isaiah 2:19; see also Joel 1:15, Zephaniah 1:14–18).

This day will *reward the righteous*. God himself will live among them; He will "assemble the exiles and those [He has] brought to grief. [He] will make the lame [His] remnant, those driven away a strong nation" (Micah 4:6–7; see also Isaiah 2:2–4 and Zechariah 2:10–13). The whole world will be made new—and freed forever from its bondage to decay!

But God's hope for the world does not gloss over individuals. He promises to make Zerubbabel like His "signet ring" and says, "I have chosen you" (Haggai 2:23). If you are God's child, He has chosen you (Ephesians 1:3–14). When everything is set free, so will you be!

God's promise for individuals does not obscure the world. A signet ring was a special stone engraved with the unique mark of a person. A king or dignitary would press the ring onto wet clay to seal a contract or document with his authority. God says Zerubbabel is His signet ring (Haggai 2:23). Unlike King Jehoiachin, whom God exiled into Babylon, saying "even if you . . . were a signet ring on my right hand, I would still pull you off" (Jeremiah 22:24), God will use Zerubbabel to re-establish His Davidic line of kings. Page ahead to Matthew's genealogy of Jesus, and you'll find Zerubbabel's name halfway between David and the promised Messiah (Matthew 1:6–17). God's promise to Zerubbabel is not merely for Zerubbabel's sake. Through his descendent Jesus Christ, God will fix the world.

Are you caught in a rut? **God's ultimate solution is _for_ you, but God's ultimate solution is not you. It's Jesus.** You may not be able to fix your situation, but you can put your faith in the One who will. Come, Lord Jesus!



Imagine being called God's signet ring! For Zerubbabel, it means being instrumental in establishing the Davidic line that led to Jesus Christ. How might you be God's signet ring in establishing His kingdom on earth today?

What or who is your ultimate hope? How can you keep your focus on this hope, even when you are stuck in a rut?

# Day 11



My friend was moving his family to a faraway place when their car broke down. As their plans were put on hold, he wondered, *why now?* Yet, he patiently responded in faith. He posted online, "I don't know what God is up to, but I suspect it's something good!"

I admire my friend's patience, though it's one thing I won't ask God to teach me. There's only one way to learn patience: being stuck in a rut, spinning our wheels deeper into the mud. Who wants that? But if we're already there, we might as well use the opportunity to grow. Waiting is too annoying to waste.

People who are stuck have a choice. We can lash out, or we can use our frustration to improve our intimacy with God and sensitivity to others. How might we serve them? How might our stuck situations draw us together?

Malachi gets right to the point. It's been some 80 years since Haggai prophesied. The temple was now completed, but it wasn't as glorious as before. The Jews remained stuck in other ways. God hadn't freed them from the power of Persia, harvests were poor, and life continued to be difficult. Where was the glory He promised? *Why obey God if He doesn't deliver?* Judah gave up on

God. (Only the two southern tribes of Judah returned from exile; the 10 northern tribes of Israel were absorbed by their captors and disappeared as a nation.)

So God summons them to court. Malachi contains six speeches against Judah, all aimed at restoring their relationship with Him. God's people may be stuck, but they can leverage their frustration to make spiritual progress. Yes, they're stuck, but they can still move forward.

God's first speech announces His love. "'I have loved you,' says the LORD." But Judah is sceptical. *Really? We haven't seen it* (Malachi 1:2). God responds (and I paraphrase), "Here's how I loved you. You are Jacob's children, and I loved him and rejected Esau. I devastated the land of Esau's descendants. If they rebuild, I'll tear it down again. My wrath will always be upon them" (vv. 2–4).

Now we may think, *that doesn't sound like love!* It helps to remember the Edomites deserved their destruction. They turned on their brother Israel and fought against God. Whatever judgment they received, they had it coming (see Obadiah 8–14).

God doesn't give anyone less than they deserve, but He does give His children more. Much more. Judah didn't deserve God's patient forgiveness, yet He repeatedly loved and restored them. We don't know why God chose Jacob. The ultimate reason is His will: God chose him because He chose him. If you are God's child, the same is true for you. **God loves you because He loves you.** Do you doubt it? Look around. How good has God been to you?



## ThinkThrough

How do you normally respond when you are stuck in a rut: lash out in frustration or wait patiently upon the Lord? What happens after that?

Where have you seen God's love in your life? How might remembering His love help you stay faithful to Him?

# **Day** 12

**Read** Malachi 1:6–9

The most frustrating place to get stuck is in our relationships with people. It hurts, especially when those people are close to us. What causes more heartache than a cheating spouse or a contemptuous child?

God understands. He's been there. He knows how it feels to have an unfaithful spouse (Malachi 2:11). And He knows how unfair parenting can be. *Why can't I have a normal relationship with my child? How can anyone be so ungrateful?*

God begins His second speech by reminding Judah that most children honour their parents. So, *what's wrong with them?* "If I am a father, where is the honour due to me?" (1:6). Worse, it's the priests, the leaders whose one job is to worship God, "who show contempt for [His] name".

Any parent with a stubborn child is familiar with what happens next. The child concedes nothing. He claims no problem exists. He's going to make you prove it, in excruciating detail. That's exactly how the priests respond to God's charge. They defiantly meet God's gaze and ask, "How have we shown contempt for your name?" (v. 6).

God sighs and states the obvious: "By offering defiled food on my altar." The priests pretend to be offended: "How have we defiled you?" (v. 7). They're going to make God say it. So He does. *Your sacrifices are blind, lame, or diseased. You wouldn't dare treat anyone you respect like this. Yet you offer them to me!* "Try offering them to your governor! Would he be pleased with you? Would he accept you?" (v. 8).

When you're stuck with a stubborn child, it's easy to blame yourself. *What did I do wrong?* None of us are perfect, so we have said and done plenty of dumb things. But that doesn't mean your child's attitude is your fault. God is the perfect Father, yet He has children who disobey Him. A good parent is not necessarily the one with the well-behaved kids. A good parent is the one who firmly yet graciously offers his children a way home.

God pleads with Judah to face the facts. He cannot accept their insulting sacrifices, yet He's ready to forgive, if only they own up to their rebellion and seek reconciliation (v. 9). **Judah may have turned away from God, but God's door remains open for them to return. They will, however, have to enter on His righteous terms.**

Are you stuck in a relationship that has soured? It's easy to walk away, but it's better to seek reconciliation. Honestly confront, confess what you've contributed, and whenever possible, provide a path home.



What are the causes of your soured relationship? What failings must you confess to the person? What is the best outcome you could hope for? Ask God for it.

Are you giving God His due honour? What might God be asking you to do today?

# Day 13



Our modern food supply is bloodless. Many of us eat meat without butchering an animal, plucking its feathers, or hacking the fat off its bones. Our steaks come packaged in plastic, with no sign they were ever alive.

The food that God demanded was not so sanitized. He told His people to take their best animals and slay them with their own hands (Malachi 1:7–9; see Leviticus 1). Judah's place of worship was a butcher's shop, drenched in blood and the dying bleats of doomed lambs. God didn't require these sacrifices because He was a carnivore. He only "ate" the food symbolically. He demanded death because of sin.

It must have been difficult to slit the throat of a pretty little lamb. That was the point. The pain of death pressed upon God's people the gravity of their sin. It was necessary for their forgiveness.

God is love and righteousness *and life*. If this is true, then what is opposite of God also has its own logical coherence. Selfishness is sin *which is death*. **God wouldn't be true to His loving and righteous nature if He brushed aside our sin, pretending it didn't happen.**

He would violate himself, which would destroy Him and consequently everything else.

So God must forgive us without violating His character. But how? There was only one way. Someone would have to die, and that someone would have to be Him. God loved us so much that He sent "his one and only Son", the perfect lamb, to die for our sin (John 1:29; 3:16). The sacrificial lambs that God demanded were pointers to Jesus, God's ultimate sacrifice.

That's why God was outraged by Judah's shameful sacrifices—the blind, sick, and lame lambs (Malachi 1:6). They poured contempt on God's beloved Son, and foreclosed Judah's forgiveness. How could God restore them if they mocked the only path available? So God pled with them to "plead with [Him] to be gracious" (v. 9). He stood ready to forgive, if they repented and returned to Him.

Today, we no longer kill lambs to atone for our sins because Jesus, the Lamb of God, has come. The full price for sin has been paid. Like Judah, our worship also rests on sacrifice—Jesus' ultimate sacrifice— which we proclaim whenever we take the bread and the cup of the Lord's Supper. This meal provides

perspective. We may be mired in a muddled mess, but our most pressing problem has been solved. We were stuck in sin with the whole world, but Jesus died to free us if only we confess our sin and put our faith in Him. What are you waiting for?



How might people today pour contempt on God's ultimate sacrifice?

How does Jesus' sacrifice and your salvation provide a fresh perspective on the situation you're stuck in? What can you do to keep this perspective?

# Day 14

**Read** Malachi 1:10–14

Renowned theologian B. B. Warfield told his students that studying God in seminary was both a great danger and a great privilege. It was dangerous because they might get used to it and lose their appreciation for God's Word. When it's your job to study the Bible, day in and day out, God and His salvation may start to seem mundane. But what a privilege! How blessed are you if your greatest danger is that you are spending so much time learning about Jesus that you might take Him for granted!

But it's still a danger. Israel's priests offered sacrifices, day in and day out. It was their job, and it bored them. God says they might as well stop. "Oh, that one of you would shut the temple doors, so that you would not light useless fires on my altar!" (Malachi 1:10). The priests had forgotten how privileged they were. God had chosen them to lead His people in worship, to honour the one true God, whose "name will be great among the nations, from where the sun rises to where it sets" (v. 11).

And they don't care. Worse, they treat God and His worship with contempt. They "sniff at it contemptuously" and say "What a burden!" (v. 13). They promise to sacrifice a perfect lamb from the flock, but "bring injured, lame, or diseased animals" instead (vv. 13–14).

Marriage counsellors say there are few things worse than contempt. They can help couples navigate the hot emotion of anger, but when that cools into disgust and hardens into disdain, when conversations are punctuated by sarcasm and eye rolling, when spouses can't stand to be in the same room, then the couples are headed for divorce. Their only hope is to remember why they once loved and respected their spouse. So, God reminds His scornful priests, "I am a great king, and my name is to be feared among the nations" (v. 14).

When you've been stuck for a long time, and your prayers don't seem to make any difference, it's tempting to treat God with contempt. Worship can feel like a burden, something you must do on top of everything else. This is your great danger. But it's also your high privilege. You're not doomed to wallow in your stuck situation. You can break out of it as you pray, read God's Word, and gather with God's people to praise and celebrate Jesus.

I don't know how and where you are stuck. I do know, however, that **God provides you with the**

"

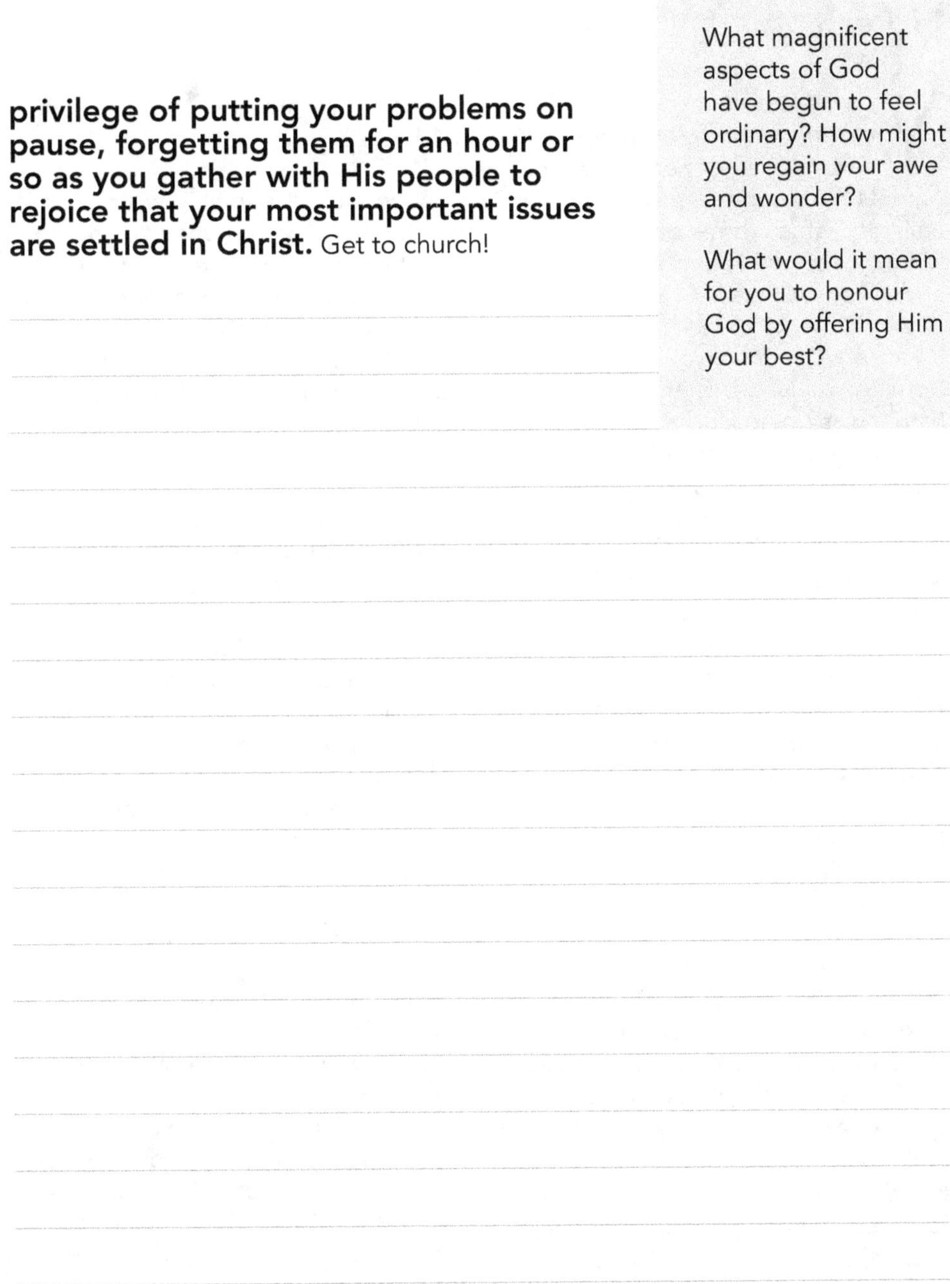

**privilege of putting your problems on pause, forgetting them for an hour or so as you gather with His people to rejoice that your most important issues are settled in Christ.** Get to church!

# Day 15

**Read** Malachi 1:10–14

You were born into a story. Your parents were doing things before you got here, and their parents before them. Your family has a history, which forms part of your identity. You are your parents' child, and always will be.

If you're a Christian, you have been born again into a better story. Your Father was doing kind and powerful things before you arrived. He has a history, which defines you. You are a child of God, and always will be.

Malachi is an important part of your Father's story. Since you are His child, it's a vital piece of your story too. Twice the Lord Almighty declares, "My name will be great among the nations" (Malachi 1:11). Because He is a "great king", His name is to be "feared among the nations" (v. 14). God will be worshiped everywhere—"from where the sun rises to where it sets"—by people from all nations (v. 11).

This worldwide worship has already begun. **God has you and me in mind when He promises that people from every race and place will praise His greatness.** Every weekend we gather with believers throughout the world—Jew and Gentile, male and female, slave and free, black, white, red, yellow, and brown—to "declare the praises of him who called you out of darkness into his wonderful light" (1 Peter 2:9).

This worldwide worship will climax in our life to come, when "a great multitude that no one could count, from every nation, tribe, people and language" will praise our glorious Lamb. We will shout, "Salvation belongs to our God, who sits on the throne, and to the Lamb" (Revelation 7:9–10).

If you follow Jesus, this is your story. Your current predicament may make it difficult for you to see this glorious future, but there's no doubt that your life will end in exaltation. You will raise your hands in triumph to praise our great King, with uncountable new best friends. All this time, when it seemed your life was stuck in neutral, you were actually moving towards this cosmic celebration. You were on the right side of history all along.

This is God's story, and He graciously invites you and me to participate. He doesn't want to hold this victory party without you. He wants you there. He wants you now. When we assemble in our humble little churches, we worship with "thousands upon thousands of angels in joyful assembly", with the whole worldwide church, with "God, the Judge of all", and with "Jesus the mediator of a new covenant"

(Hebrews 12:22–24). What a story, and it's yours!
Claim it.

# Day 16

**Read** Malachi 2:1–3

A crowd gathered in a Beijing intersection to watch two middle-aged Chinese women screaming at each other. One had pedalled into the other's bike, but at this point it was impossible to tell who was at fault. It didn't matter. Each was determined to save face; neither was about to back down.

It was an ugly, unfortunate scene, yet the two ladies were onto something. Their passion for honour is something God understands. The Lord Almighty continues His rebuke of the priests for dishonouring Him. If they do not change, God will "curse [their] blessings". Indeed, "I have already cursed them, because you have not resolved to honour me" (Malachi 2:2). This line in Hebrew literally reads, "because you do not set your heart to give glory to my name."

The Hebrew word for glory is *kābôd*. It comes from the Hebrew root, *kbd*, which means to be heavy or weighty. We honour God by declaring His worth, then living out that belief. The priests did neither. This was ironic since the "glory (*kābôd*) of Yahweh" had once filled the temple. The splendour of God's glory had shone so brightly at the first temple's grand opening that the priests could not perform their duties (2 Chronicles 5:14). Now they were once again not doing their job, but for the opposite reason.

They didn't respect the dignity, the gravitas of God.

So God promises to shame them. In Leviticus 4:4–12, He had instructed the priests to sprinkle the sacrificial animal's blood and burn its fat on the altar of the tabernacle (and later temple), then take the unclean residue that was left, including "the internal organs and intestines", outside the camp and burn it. Now God vows to rub their faces in it: "I will smear on your faces the dung from your festival sacrifices" (Malachi 2:3). Since the priests had refused to worship God rightly, He would make them ceremonially unclean, disqualifying them from serving at all. They had dishonoured God; He would dishonour them.

When we're confronted by our sins, we often look for ways to save face. We make excuses or blame others in a desperate attempt to preserve our dignity. But God's honour matters more than ours. **Instead of trying to control what others think or say about us, we can set our hearts to tell God and them what we know He's worth.** Let's lift our praise, and live our days, to the glory of God.

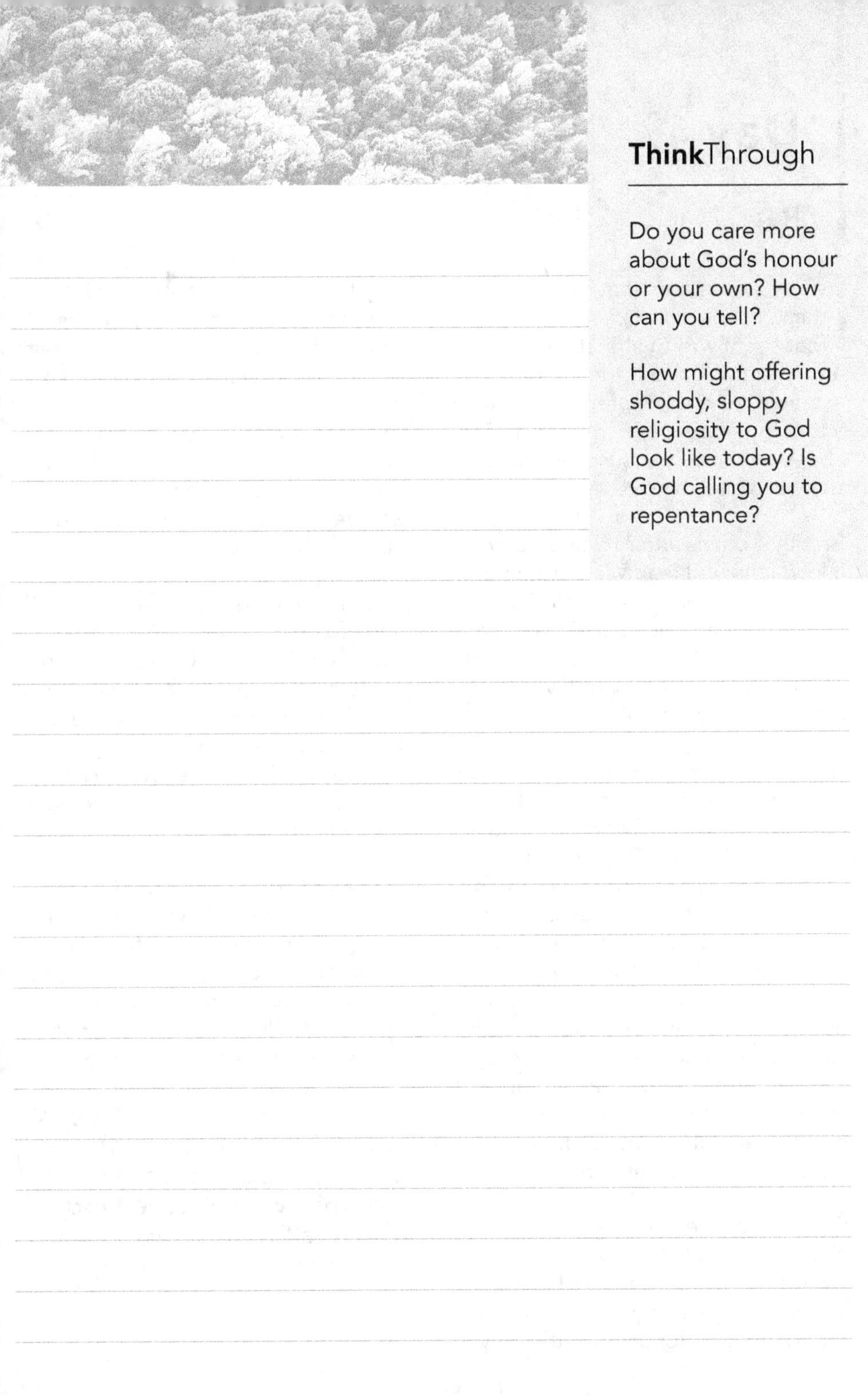

## **Think**Through

Do you care more about God's honour or your own? How can you tell?

How might offering shoddy, sloppy religiosity to God look like today? Is God calling you to repentance?

**Read** Malachi 2:4–5

I enjoy statements that make me think. I especially like statements that seem wrong at first glance, until you think about them. For example, take this statement I read in a theology book: "We must fear God above all things because we may love Him above all things".

Isn't that backwards? I'd understand if love followed fear. We must love God lest He damn us to hell. But how does fear follow love? We love God for His sake. Why should we fear losing the opportunity to love Him? It's for Him anyway.

God explains why. He tells the priests that His warnings of shame and cursing are because of His covenant with them (Malachi 2:4). He yearns for a relationship of love, and not for His benefit, but all for theirs. God's covenant is "a covenant of life and peace" (v. 5). The Hebrew word for peace is *shalom*. It means both absence of conflict and satisfying success, both peace and prosperity. This promise is so central to God's covenant with Israel that Jews still greet one another with *shalom aleichem*, "peace unto you."

God presents each of us with a choice: will we live for ourselves, or will we die to ourselves and follow Jesus? It may seem paradoxical, but losing our lives for Jesus is the only way to find life (Matthew 16:24–25). When we give ourselves to Jesus, turning from sin and putting our faith in Him alone, we get our lives back. We can now exult in the freedom that only union with Christ can bring. As Jesus prayed, "this is eternal life: that they know you, the only true God, and Jesus Christ, whom you have sent" (John 17:3).

Our choice is between life and death, and life only comes from loving our triune God. And so God's covenant of life and peace calls for "reverence" and "awe" (Malachi 2:5). We must fear God because we may love Him. We fear God because loving Him is life, and we would die if He took our opportunity away.

It's natural to fear the people and the problems that have caused our predicament. It's normal to wake up in the middle of the night and worry about the many ways our problem may end badly. We'd be fools not to fear. But we'd be bigger fools if those fears weren't dwarfed by the far weightier fear of God. **We can't control the outcome of our situation, but we can decide whether we will love God above all things.** Let your fear that you won't drive you to Him.

What does "rever-
ence" and "awe"
mean to you?

Whom or what do
you fear? What can
you do to put your
fears in their proper
order?

# Day 18



A friend offered to pray with me about the situation I was feeling stuck in. I didn't want to. I still don't. There had been a time when prayer could have made a difference. Now it was too late. The die was cast, the horse was out of the barn—pick your favourite metaphor— the train was down the tracks. No one could put Humpty Dumpty together again.

My pain was great because my situation had once held so much promise. As God closes His speech against the priests, He feels the same way about them. The priests hailed from the tribe of Levi, who had taught the people well. "True instruction was in his mouth . . . He walked with me in peace and uprightness, and turned many from sin" (Malachi 2:6). But now the decadent priests have "turned from the way and by [their] teaching have caused many to stumble; [they] have violated the covenant with Levi" (v. 8). God will shame them before the people "because [they] have not followed [His] ways but have shown partiality in matters of the law" (v. 9).

We're not sure what the priests were teaching or how they were corrupting justice, but it's no surprise that their detestable worship of God would bleed into their mistreatment of others. It's impossible to despise God and yet love those who are made in His image. **Our attitude towards**

## God inevitably determines our affection for others.

God's warning to the priests also means it's never too late to do what's right. The situation might seem hopeless—at least in the short term—but we can still obey God, simply because it's the right thing to do. The priests could repent and do their jobs with passion, for no other reason than "the lips of a priest ought to preserve knowledge, because he is the messenger of the Lord Almighty and people seek instruction from his mouth" (v. 7).

It might be too late to turn the nation back to God, but godly priests could still save someone. And even if it's too late to make a difference in anyone's life, godly priests could still honour God by teaching and obeying His truth. It's never too late for that.

I'm sorry for my stuck situation, and for yours. But this is no time for despair. Let's do what's right regardless, let's bow our knees in prayer. No mess that makes us more reliant on God is ever wasted.

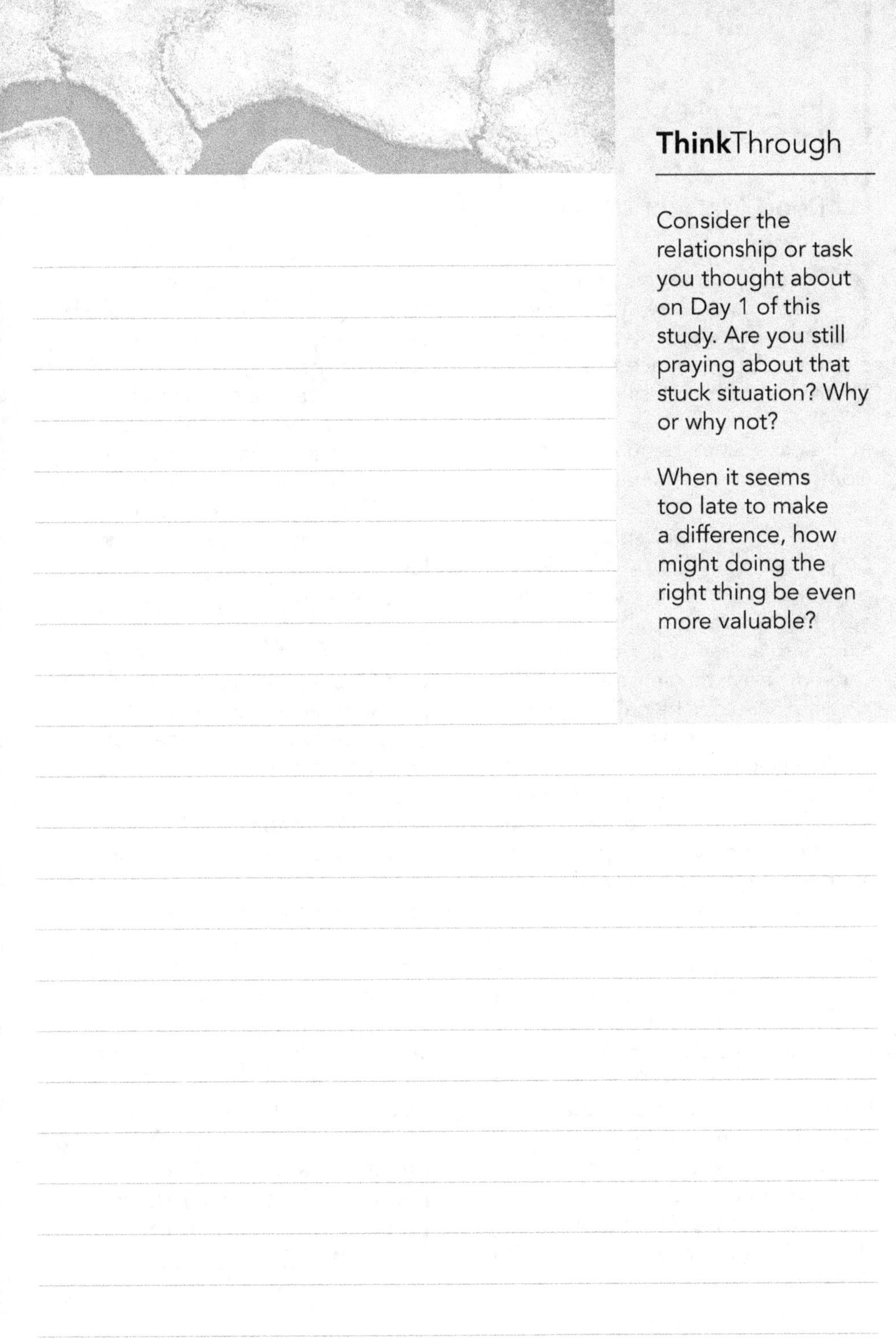

ThinkThrough

Consider the relationship or task you thought about on Day 1 of this study. Are you still praying about that stuck situation? Why or why not?

When it seems too late to make a difference, how might doing the right thing be even more valuable?

# **Day** 19

**Read** Malachi 2:10–12

Chen laughs at his pornography addiction. Sure, it's technically a sin, but whom does it hurt? Well, every sin does violence to someone. There are no victimless sins.

In this case, Chen dehumanises women, turning them into objects of sexual pleasure. He dehumanises himself. Chen is being played by pornographers who make money off him with fees and ads. He's an easy mark because he has reduced himself to a snarl of illicit desires. Chen destroys the self-esteem of his wife. She cries herself to sleep, knowing she will never measure up to his online fantasies. He corrodes the trust of his children, who sense something isn't right between mum and dad. He plays the hypocrite at church, pretending all is well at home. And the cancer spreads.

God opens His third speech by noting that sin victimises and contaminates both the sinner and those around him. The detestable worship of the priests has spread to the people, who have "desecrated the sanctuary the Lᴏʀᴅ loves by marrying women who worship a foreign god" (Malachi 2:11). The common people figure that if the priests don't take God seriously, why should they? So they go to bed with idolaters.

Israelite men didn't go looking for foreign gods. They were enticed by women whose sexual charms and social connections to local merchants and trade cartels promised to make them happy and rich. Lust led to idolatry, which stoked lust, which heightened idolatry in a self-perpetuating vicious cycle. Idolatry wasn't the goal. It was the price of lust, which the men gladly—and tragically—paid.

Their sin violates their covenant with God and also breaks faith with one another. Malachi asks, "Why do we profane the covenant of our ancestors by being unfaithful to one another?" (v. 10). Idolaters not only destroy their relationship with God, they also ravage the community they belong to. They incite God's wrath upon the whole lot.

God will not share His glory with another (Isaiah 42:8). Whoever splits his devotion between God and idols will be removed "from the tents of Jacob—even though he brings an offering to the Lᴏʀᴅ Almighty" (Malachi 2:12). **Nothing compensates for the sin of idolatry. Our only move is to smash the idols and return to God.**

If you're stuck in a rut, it could be because someone has broken faith with you, and they've done so because they first broke faith with God. You can stop the cycle by not perpetuating idolatry and injustice. With God's help, you can start new, virtuous cycles of holiness and peace. Loving God and loving others are contagious.



Identify one sin that you've noticed in yourself or others. Who are its victims?

What idols do you need to destroy? How might this improve the situation you're stuck in?

# Day 20



Tom and Sue cohabited for several years. Then Sue became a Christian. She and Tom, who already was a believer, decided they should marry. That's when the fighting began. This puzzled them. Why did they get along when they were living in sin, and begin to fight only when they determined to obey God?

Here's why: Satan leaves us alone when we're doing what he wants. He only troubles us when he's afraid, and few things scare him more than a husband and wife who love and respect each other. Their bond of devotion creates strong families with "godly offspring" that threaten Satan's schemes (Malachi 2:15). Are you married? Buckle up! Satan wants to destroy what you've got.

God tells Judah there are two ways to be unfaithful. They can break faith with God through idolatry, and they can break faith with others. In this case, through divorce. Tragically, they've done both. God doesn't accept their worship or answer their prayers because they've divorced their wives (v. 13). "You have been unfaithful to her, though she is your partner, the wife of your marriage covenant" (v. 14).

The Hebrew term for partner comes from a root word that describes the seam in the tabernacle curtains (Exodus 26:3–11). As the curtains were sewn together permanently, so a husband and wife unite their lives and bodies in an unbreakable "one flesh" bond (Genesis 2:24). Marriage isn't a contract that can be ripped up when one partner disappoints. It's a sacred covenant between a man, a woman, and God (Malachi 2:14).

The Hebrew text of verse 16 is difficult to interpret. It could mean that God hates divorce, as the King James Version says. Or it could mean, as the New International and English Standard Versions read, that the man who divorces his wife claims that he hates her. Either way, God declares that the person who divorces his wife, except for adultery or abandonment (Matthew 19:1–12; 1 Corinthians 7:15), "does violence to the one he should protect" (Malachi 2:16). Our home should be the safest place in the world. When that becomes the scene of emotional and spiritual violence, what could be worse?

God wants us to avoid such trauma. He warns, "So be on your guard, and do not be unfaithful" (v. 16). Don't presume your wife knows that you love her, or your husband knows that you respect him. Tell them. Build hedges to protect your marriage. Make each other a priority.

Godly, life-giving marriages do not happen naturally, especially with an enemy prowling to rip them apart. **Marriage takes work, disciplined focus, and extra helpings of forgiveness. It is worth the effort.**



For those who are married, what is one thing you could do to improve your marriage? How might you protect it from the enemy?

If you're not married, how could you pray for or support married people in your church? If you intend to be married, how might you prepare for marriage?

**Read** Malachi 2:17

Teenagers can be exhausting. They are developing a necessary sense of self, but they tend to interpret life only by how it affects them. Your 16-year-old may carelessly make a mess in the kitchen or forget to do his chores, assuming that someone else—usually his mum—will clean up after him. Yet he'll quickly take offense if his mum raises her voice to correct him. *Why is everyone so mean?*

God found Judah to be exhausting. He begins His fourth speech by saying they have wearied Him with their cynical complaints: "All who do evil are good in the eyes of the Lord, and he is pleased with them", and "Where is the God of justice?" (Malachi 2:17). Like a spoiled teenager, Judah saw everything through the prism of self. They wondered why God tolerated so much sin in others. Why didn't He punish the disobedient and bless the righteous, as He promised? Judah should be careful what they wish for. When the God of justice appears, things may not go as they expect.

Being in a rut can be exhausting, to us and to others. It's easy to develop a skewed view of the world. We've been mired in the same place for so long that we've forgotten how things look from other perspectives. We only see how this or that affects us.

We turn casual conversations into referendums on our unjust plight. We fill the open spaces of our day with fretting, and mull over our options whenever there's a lull. We can't even pray for long. Our minds slip back into well-worn ruts of worry. *Why are they so mean?*

People in ruts often need sympathy, but also a reality check. We may feel certain that we're right, but we need to remember that right and wrong do not depend on us. That's important, because the vantage point from our ditch is bound to be distorted.

Thankfully, God has not left us to figure life out for ourselves. **His Word tells us what is right and wrong, and what He expects from us.** His Word may be tough to hear, especially when we're used to seeing things our way. It may not even feel right, because it rubs against our ingrained patterns of self-interest. When that happens, remember our feelings are corrupted by our fallen nature. We must trust the God who made us. He knows what's best.

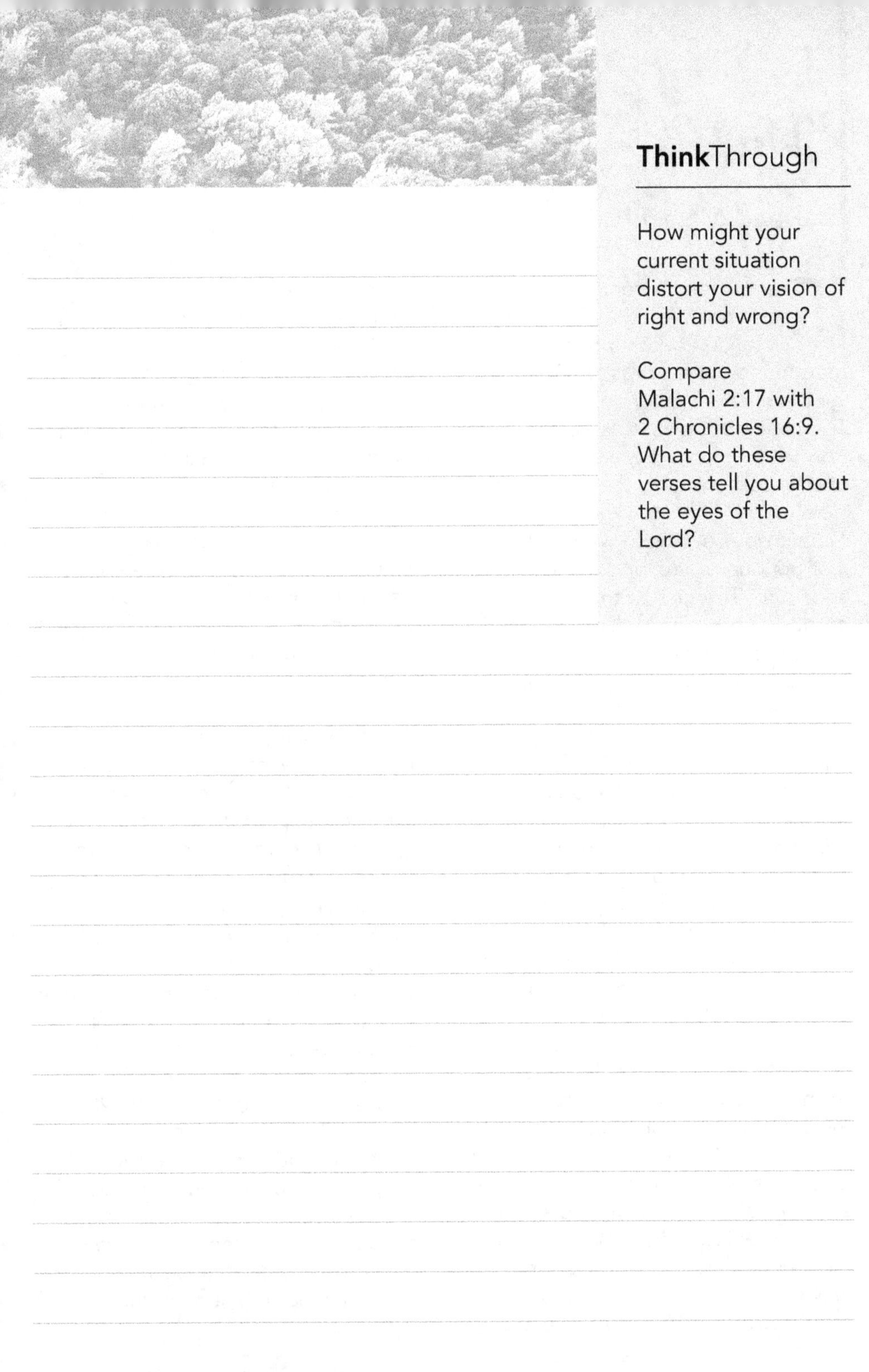


ThinkThrough

How might your
current situation
distort your vision of
right and wrong?

Compare
Malachi 2:17 with
2 Chronicles 16:9.
What do these
verses tell you about
the eyes of the
Lord?

# **Day** 22



The written instructions for staining a fibreglass door were detailed and daunting. They mentioned cloths, rags and foam, synthetic and natural bristle brushes. They spelt out what to stain first, how long to let it dry, and when to rub against and with the grain. I was paralysed by doubt. *Why did I think I could do this?* Then I watched an instructional video, and my fears subsided. The man in the video carried out the instructions perfectly. He embodied the rules. If I followed his example, my door would come out fine.

Judah asks, "Where is the God of justice?" (Malachi 2:17). God doesn't answer with a checklist or itemised instructions. He answers with a person. "I will send my messenger, who will prepare the way before me. Then suddenly the Lord you are seeking will come to his temple; the messenger of the covenant, whom you desire, will come" (3:1).

Who is this messenger? It refers to three increasingly important individuals. The first messenger is the prophet Malachi who wrote this book (the phrase "my messenger" is spelt *malaki* in Hebrew). The second messenger is John the Baptist, whom God would later send to clear the way for Israel's Messiah. Jesus told the crowds that Malachi 3:1 refers to John, who is the greatest of all the prophets (see Matthew 11:7–14).

The ultimate messenger is Jesus. He is "the Lord you are seeking", "the God of justice", and "the messenger of the covenant". Jesus perfectly embodies justice and love, truth and grace (John 1:14). He doesn't hold His righteousness over our heads as a reason to condemn us. Rather He uses His justice to fulfil the demands of Israel's Mosaic covenant and to graciously establish His new covenant.

Jesus himself is the new covenant. He is "a covenant for the people and a light for the Gentiles" (Isaiah 42:6). **Jesus keeps both ends of this covenant, performing God's promises and ours.** God promised to save and we promised to obey, so Jesus did both when He offered His perfect life on our behalf. We remember our reliance on Him when we partake in the Lord's Supper. Jesus said, "This cup is the new covenant in my blood, which is poured out for you" (Luke 22:20).

Have you noticed that people like to give advice when you're in a rut? *Do this! Do that!* Sometimes their suggestions contradict, and we don't know what to do. Maybe we should put away the detailed instructions,

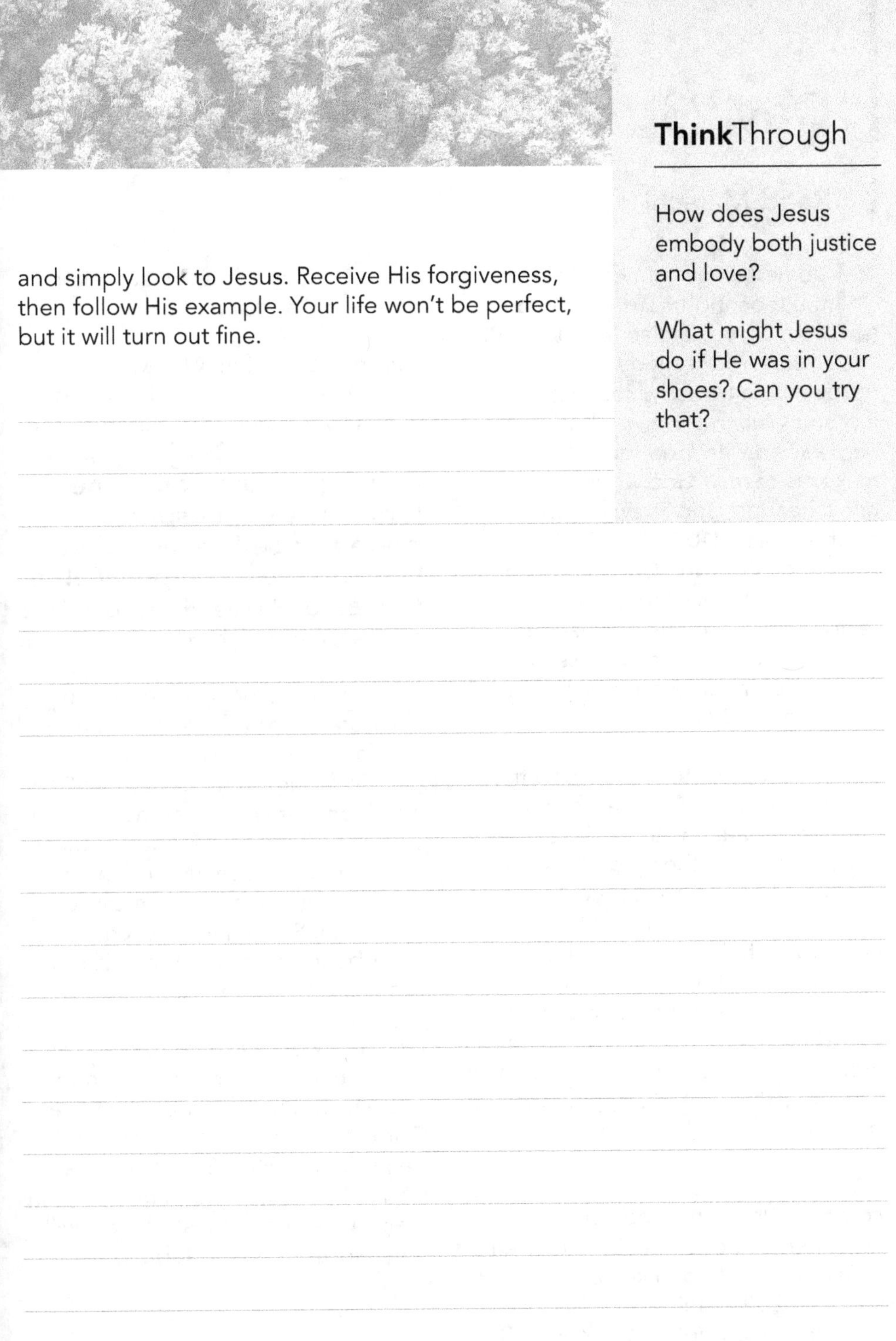

and simply look to Jesus. Receive His forgiveness, then follow His example. Your life won't be perfect, but it will turn out fine.



How does Jesus embody both justice and love?

What might Jesus do if He was in your shoes? Can you try that?

# Day 23



Job had an airtight case. He was the most righteous person on earth. God said so (see Job 1:8). Yet he suffered tragedy after unspeakable tragedy. Job wasn't just stuck in a rut; He was buried. So he pleaded with God for a chance to make his case. If God would only give him a hearing, Job knew he would clear his name (10:2–7; 13:22–23; 23:1–7; 31:35). Then God arrived in a storm, and blew Job away. Job realised his righteousness had no claim on God, and he confessed, "I despise myself and repent in dust and ashes" (42:6).

Judah knew the story of Job, so they should have known better than to beg for a hearing with God. Yet they cried, "Where is the God of justice?" (Malachi 2:17). God answered by promising to send a messenger to clear away their evil debris, then "suddenly the Lord you are seeking will come" (3:1). But don't clap just yet. The Lord of love accepts us as we are, but He loves us too much to allow us to stay that way. His appearance is going to hurt.

"Who can endure the day of his coming? Who can stand when he appears?" No one. The Lord himself is "a refiner's fire or a launderer's soap" (v. 2). The furnace of His love will refine and purify us, burning off our impurities so that what's left is pure "gold and silver" (v. 3).

Judgment isn't fun. Who wants to learn that what they liked most about themselves is actually dross that must be melted away? **But judgment that refines is a compliment. It means that, despite our pride and selfishness, God believes we are too valuable to waste.** He sees the gold that we can become, and thinks we're worth it.

When Jesus returns, He will judge our works, proclaim His forgiveness, and forever change us. Then we "will bring offerings in righteousness", offerings that are "acceptable to the LORD" (vv. 3–4). Meanwhile, we must prepare for the coming judgment. Our rut may not have been caused by our sin. Sin might not even be a contributing factor. But we still have some sins to repent from.

Like Job, we may yearn to plead our case with God. That's fine, as long as we keep the proper perspective. Our job isn't to judge God; we will be judged by Him. So we confess with Job: "But he knows the way that I take; when he has tested me, I will come forth as gold" (Job 23:10).

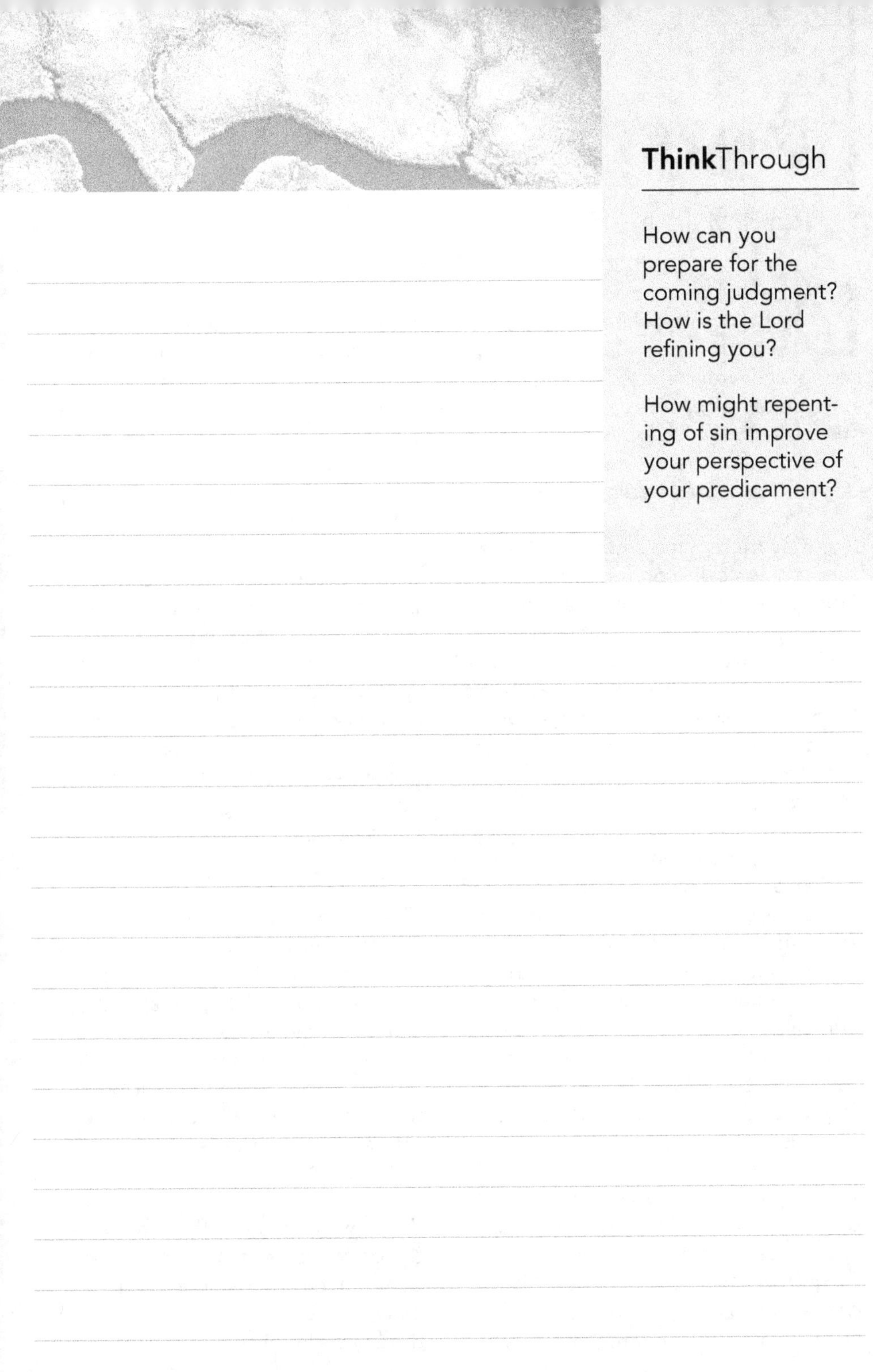


ThinkThrough

How can you
prepare for the
coming judgment?
How is the Lord
refining you?

How might repent-
ing of sin improve
your perspective of
your predicament?

# Day 24

**Read** Malachi 3:5

Do you know a good person who does not know Jesus? She isn't religious, yet she gets along well with others. She's quick to hug, encourage, and sit quietly with friends who are struggling. Everyone loves her, but she doesn't yet love Jesus. How do we explain this?

She may be a prime example of what theologians call "common grace." God the Creator bestows natural blessings on everyone. In her case, she may have received extra helpings of kindness and generosity. We thank God for her sunny personality—we need more friends like her—while we pray that she will come to love the One who made her so loveable.

Of course, she might also be nice because she doesn't yet have a reason not to be. It's easy to smile when the world smiles back at you. It's not until we feel threatened that we show our true selves. If we love ourselves most, we'll lash out at those who want to take us down. If we love Jesus most, we'll pray for grace to forgive and "do good to those who hate [us]" (Luke 6:27).

There is an unbreakable bond between our relationship with God and our relationship with people. **Our love for God determines our love for people.** Malachi lists a number of sinners that blatantly abuse others: "adulterers and perjurers . . . those who defraud labourers of their wages, who oppress the widows and the fatherless, and deprive the foreigners among you of justice." All these abusers have one thing in common: they do not fear the LORD Almighty (Malachi 3:5).

Why does idolatry inevitably produce injustice? Because idolaters ultimately worship themselves. They are god, and they use their idol to get more of what they want. No one worships an idol for its own sake, but only for the power or pleasure it promises them. It's a short step from using idols to using people. Indeed, it's impossible to live for ourselves and not harm others.

The influence runs in the other direction too. An idol asks more from us until it finally demands more than we can give. So, we steal from others to give to the idol, to keep the goodies coming. In this battle of the gods, both us and the idol fight for dominance until we destroy each other. Neither of us is God, so we both fall.

When we're in a rut, there are many things we can't control. But we can control what's most important—we can choose whom we'll worship. Fear the LORD Almighty.

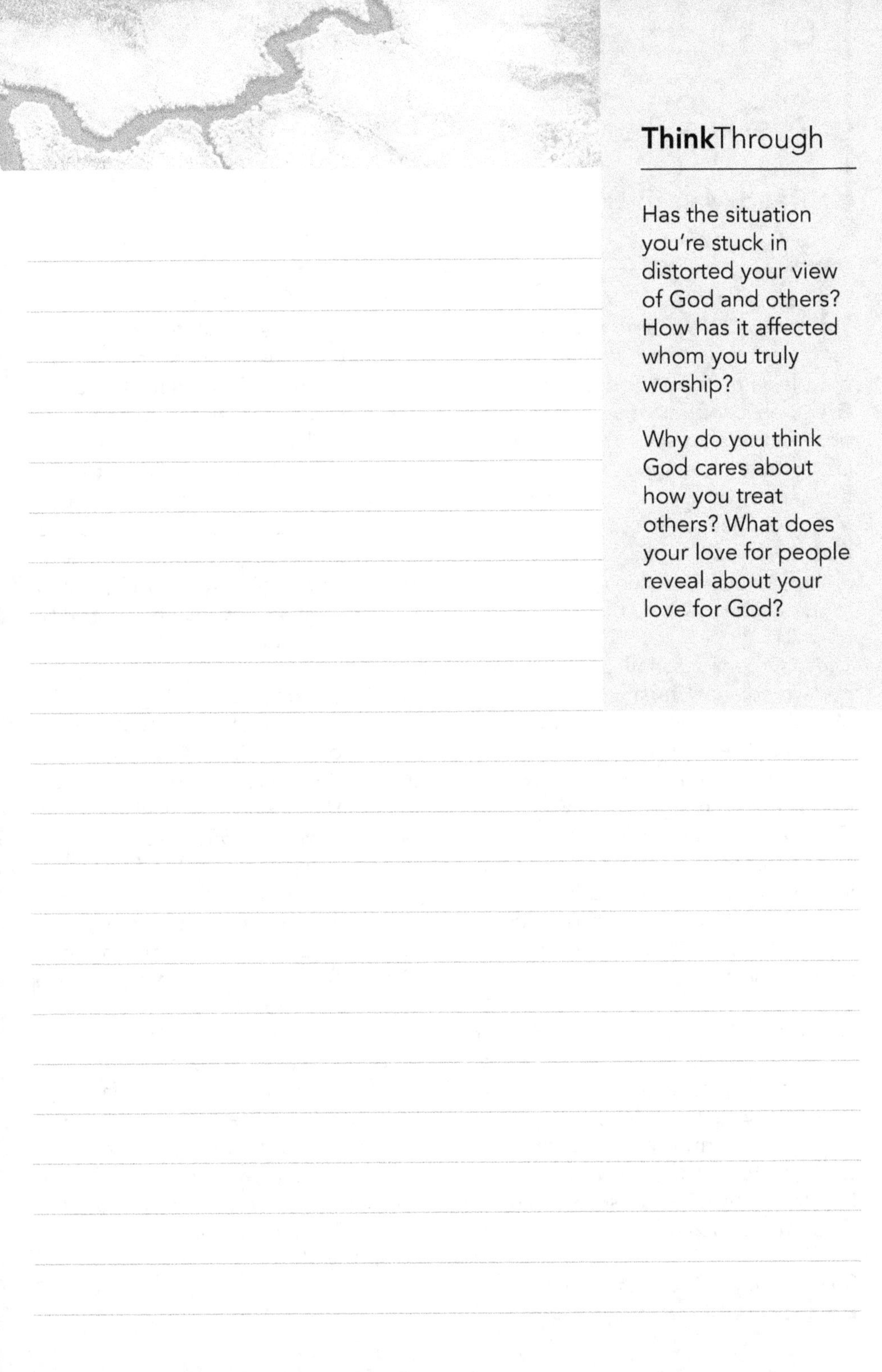

## ThinkThrough

Has the situation you're stuck in distorted your view of God and others? How has it affected whom you truly worship?

Why do you think God cares about how you treat others? What does your love for people reveal about your love for God?

# **Day** 25



The ancient philosopher Heraclitus said, "No man ever steps in the same river twice for it's not the same river and he's not the same man." Subsequent Greek philosophers made the same observation that everything on earth is constantly changing. This worried them, so several concluded there must be a heavenly, eternal realm that doesn't change at all. Only this higher, static world can give meaning to our unstable world of flux.

These Greek ideas influenced how many medieval Christians read Malachi 3:6, "I the LORD do not change." They surmised that because God exists in the heavenly realm, He must not change in any way. God exists in immutable, blissful self-contemplation. He does not act in time, because that would be a change. Earthly people may change in relation to Him, but God himself never moves.

Contemporary theologians note that this interpretation seems to view God as dead. If God never acts, how is He alive? They also rightly say this isn't the God of Scripture. God promises to return to His people who return to Him (Malachi 3:7). This sounds like a God on the move.

So what does God mean when He declares, "I the LORD do not change"? What is it that doesn't change? His *nature*. God's actions change precisely because His nature doesn't. God is both righteous and compassionate, so He sends the prophet Jonah to warn Nineveh that He will destroy them unless they repent. When they listen to Jonah and do repent, it's that same righteous and compassionate nature that causes God to relent and spare them (Jonah 1:2; 3:10). God is free to change course because His character remains constant.

God's character is unchangingly faithful. He is faithful because He is the powerful "LORD Almighty" (Malachi 3:7). We've seen this name a lot in Haggai and Malachi. It occurs in Malachi 55 times, nearly half of its use in the entire Old Testament. Judah had no army, so God repeatedly tells them that He is the "LORD Almighty" which means "Yahweh of Armies." Heaven's armies are on their side.

God is also faithful because He is love. It is because of His unchanging love that "you, the descendants of Jacob, are not destroyed" (v. 6). He stands ready to receive us the moment we repent. "'Return to me, and I will return to you,' says the LORD Almighty" (v. 7).

Are you stuck because you have turned away from God? Or has the situation you're stuck in pushed you further away? Your life may have changed dramatically, but one thing hasn't. **God's faithful character cannot change. He is as powerful and loving today as He's ever been.** The Greeks got something right. Our world of flux is frightening. We need someone as solid and unchanging as a rock. You've got one. Run to Him.



Write down all of God's qualities that you can think of.

Pick one. How might this unchanging perfection encourage you?

# Day 26



An old friend called last night. He was stuck, and needed someone to talk to. His heart had been shattered, and he said he was holding on to the last piece. He had been mistreated by others, and to be fair, he had sinned against them. I mostly listened, and tried to empathise with him. He was stuck so deep that he probably wouldn't make it all the way out in this lifetime. But he could make a good start, and experience freedom and joy, if he received Jesus' forgiveness and returned to the Lord.

In God's fifth speech, He tells Judah they have a decision to make. They could continue spinning their wheels deeper into the mud, or they could return to Him. They ask, "How are we to return?" (Malachi 3:7). God says they should keep His decrees, and they could start with bringing the "tithes and offerings" He had commanded (v. 8).

God doesn't need their money; He wants them. By giving their offerings, they are giving themselves to the Lord. Jesus says, "For where your treasure is, there your heart will be also" (Matthew 6:21). Our heart follows our treasure. We give money to what we love. By withholding their wealth, the stingy Israelites rob God and declare they only care about themselves (Malachi 3:9).

God dares Judah to test Him. "Bring the whole tithe into the storehouse . . . and see if I will not throw open the floodgates of heaven and pour out so much blessing that there will not be room enough to store it" (v. 10). God had made a covenant with Israel, in which He promised to bless the nation in every material way when they obeyed and to curse them if they disobeyed (see Deuteronomy 28). He urges them to keep their end of the covenant, and see if He doesn't keep His. "Then all the nations will call you blessed, for yours will be a delightful land" (Malachi 3:12).

This promise does not apply directly to us today. We have a new covenant, in which God has promised to "meet all [our] needs according to the riches of his glory in Christ Jesus" (Philippians 4:19). Not all our greeds, but all our needs. Our offerings are an expression of our faith. We trust God to take care of us. **Our offerings are an expression of our gratitude. We delight to give back to the One who gave himself for us.** It's easy to tell whether our hearts have returned to the Lord Almighty. Follow the money. That's where "your heart will be also" (Matthew 6:21).

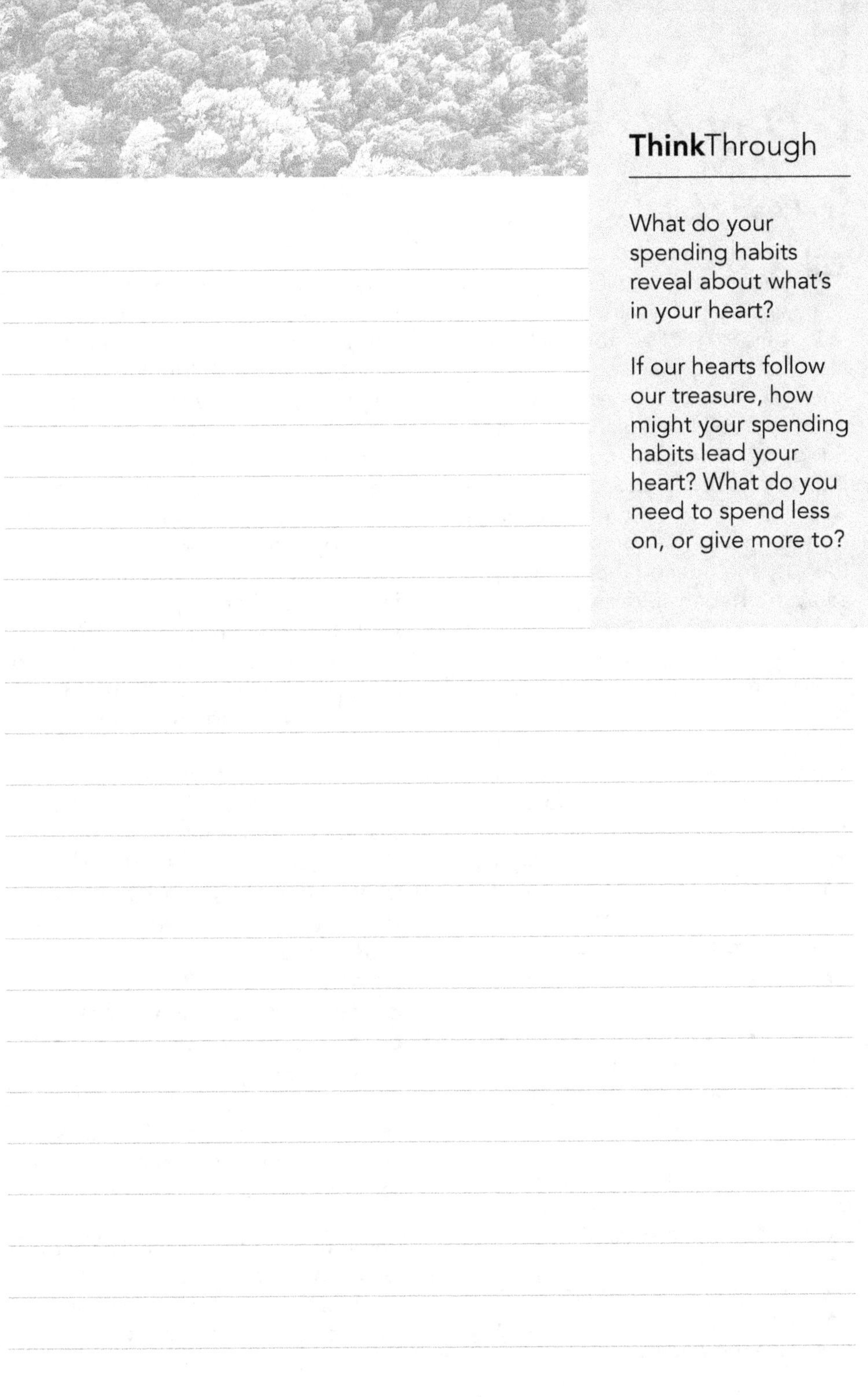

ThinkThrough

What do your
spending habits
reveal about what's
in your heart?

If our hearts follow
our treasure, how
might your spending
habits lead your
heart? What do you
need to spend less
on, or give more to?

# Day 27

**Read** Malachi 3:13–18

This is not how Kwame envisioned his life would turn out. He had led the pack on life's fast track, excelling in school and business, until he refused to compromise his allegiance to Jesus. Suddenly he was an outcast in an industry he had once dominated. He was startled by how swiftly colleagues turned on him. He complained to friends, and noticed them pulling away. He began spiralling into gloom.

Judah wasn't just spiralling downwards, they had already reached bottom. God begins His sixth and final speech by quoting their cynical words, "It is futile to serve God. What do we gain by carrying out his requirements and going about like mourners before the Lord Almighty?" (Malachi 3:14). They believed God hadn't kept His end of the covenant. They obeyed Him, and got nothing. Yet "evildoers prosper, and even when they put God to the test, they get away with it" (v. 15). Their neighbours tested God's patience through disobedience, and yet weren't punished for it.

Judah was stuck in despair. Most of them had given up on serving God and obeying Him. Most, but not all. A beam of light pierces the gloom. "Then those who feared the Lord talked with each other, and the Lord listened and heard. A scroll of remembrance was written in his presence concerning those who feared the Lord and honoured his name" (v. 16). A faithful remnant remained, and they found each other. They didn't waste energy complaining about the injustice of their plight. They focused on the positive. They encouraged each other by writing down for posterity the names of those who had been faithful and what they had done. And God, who once seemed distant, showed He had been paying attention all along. He "listened and heard" (v. 16). And promised to act.

In the short run, anything can happen. We may suffer for following Jesus. But the promise of the long view is guaranteed. **On the day of judgment, God promises that "you will again see the distinction between the righteous and the wicked, between those who serve God and those who do not" (v. 18).** Then you "will be [His] treasured possession". God will spare us from condemnation, "just as a father has compassion and spares his son who serves him" (v. 17).

Has your allegiance to Jesus cost you relationships or opportunities? Do you feel the world is against you? You are not alone. God sees you. And

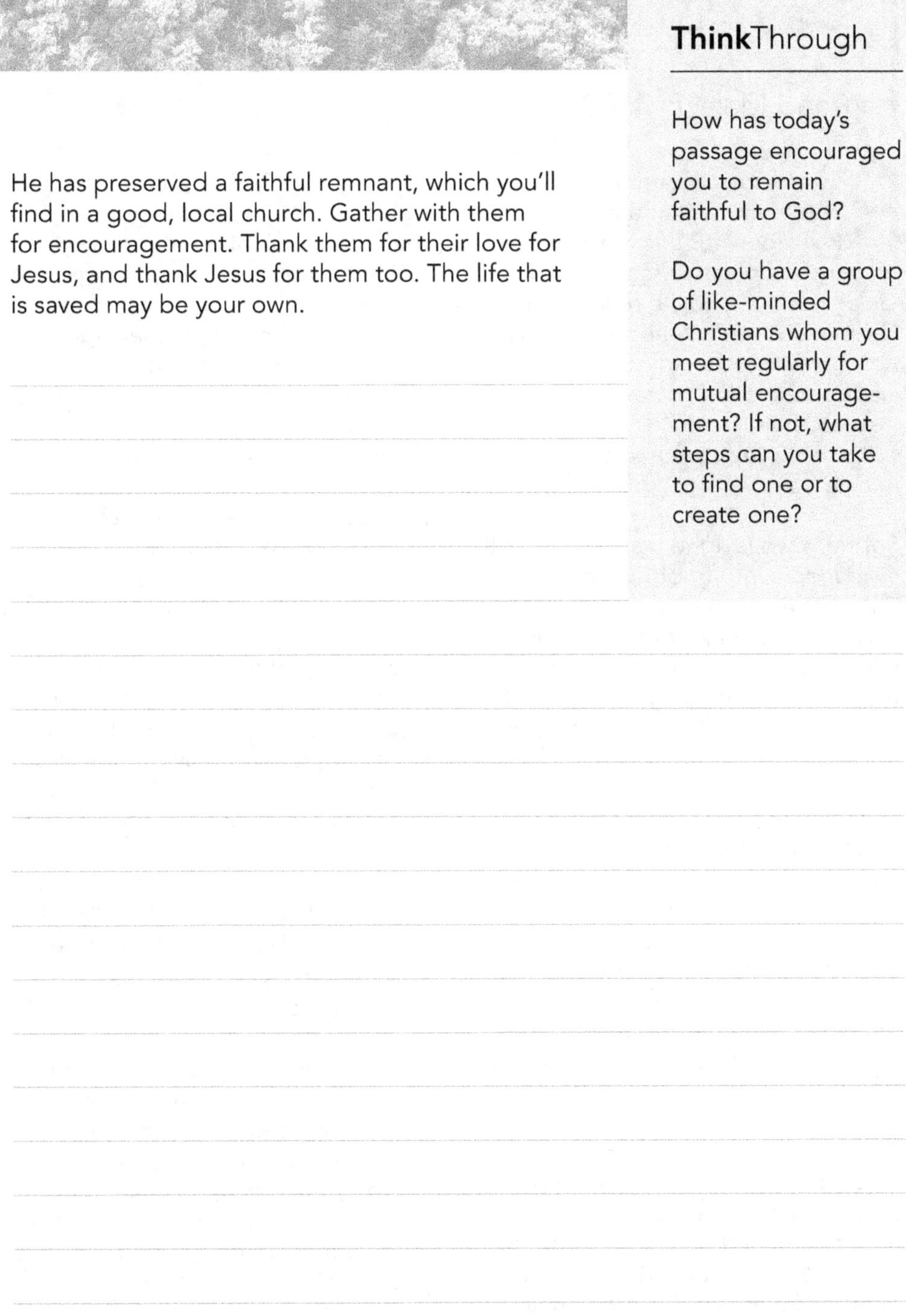

He has preserved a faithful remnant, which you'll find in a good, local church. Gather with them for encouragement. Thank them for their love for Jesus, and thank Jesus for them too. The life that is saved may be your own.



How has today's passage encouraged you to remain faithful to God?

Do you have a group of like-minded Christians whom you meet regularly for mutual encouragement? If not, what steps can you take to find one or to create one?

# Day 28

**Read** Malachi 4:1–3

Russian novelist Aleksandr Solzhenitsyn won the Nobel Prize for writing against his country's oppressive regime. In *The Gulag Archipelago*, he reflected on his imprisonment in labour camps and noted it was too simplistic to say he was good and his captors were bad. Instead, "the line dividing good and evil cuts through the heart of every human being".

Solzhenitsyn is right. It's hard for us to sort people into good and bad bins. The best are bound to disappoint, and the worst may yet surprise. It's hard for us, but not for Jesus. He will expertly separate the sheep from the goats on the day He returns to judge the world (Matthew 25:31–46).

God ends His final speech by warning that the day of the Lord will "burn like a furnace. All the arrogant and every evildoer will be stubble . . . Not a root or a branch will be left to them" (Malachi 4:1). What horror of having all that you worked for, day after day, year after year, reduced to dust! Worse, the wicked themselves will become "ashes under the soles" of the righteous (v. 3).

God ends Malachi as He began (1:1–5), promising judgment on the wicked and rescue for those "who revere my name" (4:2). For the latter, "the sun of righteousness will rise with healing in its rays" (v. 2). The phrase "sun of righteousness" appears only here in the Bible. It might refer to Yahweh, who is "a sun and shield" (Psalm 84:11). The Hebrew term for rays can also mean wings, so the phrase might be inspired by carvings of winged suns, or outstretched eagles overlaid on suns, which were common in the Ancient Near East. These pictures symbolised the gods' supposed protection and deliverance of their worshippers. As David prayed to the true God: "Hide me in the shadow of your wings" (Psalm 17:8).

The sun of righteousness is fulfilled in Jesus. When John the Baptist was born, his father prophesied that he would prepare the way for the Lord, who as "the rising sun will come to us from heaven, to shine on those living in darkness and in the shadow of death, to guide our feet into the path of peace" (Luke 1:78–79). **Jesus is the Son whose outstretched, cruciform arms heal us by atoning for our sin.**

The line between good and evil runs through every human heart, so the final sorting doesn't depend on us becoming good enough. We can't. The only goodness that matters belongs to the Son of righteousness. His goodness becomes ours when we put our faith in Him. Are you in Him?

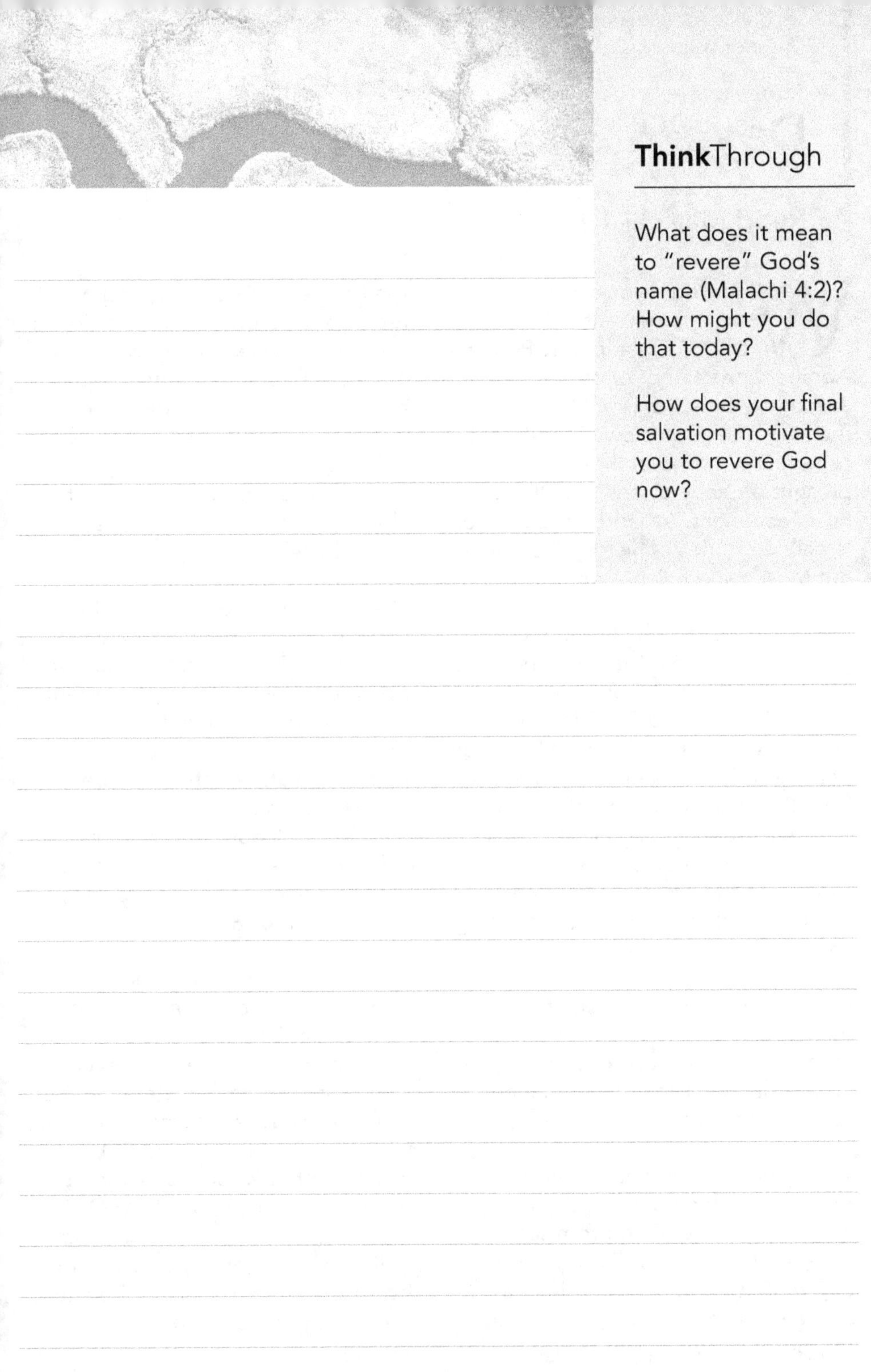

ThinkThrough

What does it mean to "revere" God's name (Malachi 4:2)? How might you do that today?

How does your final salvation motivate you to revere God now?

# **Day** 29



Who would you say is the most important person in the Old Testament? Perhaps Abraham, the father of our faith? Or Jacob, the father of Israel? Or David, the king after God's own heart? May I suggest it's none of these? Our present passage closes the Old, or First Testament. As God looks back on Israel's centuries of history, He singles out Moses and Elijah. *Why them?*

Moses represents the law that God gave to His people "at Horeb [Mount Sinai] for all Israel." God gave them these "decrees and laws" immediately after delivering them from the bondage of Egypt (Malachi 4:4). Their exodus from Egypt united the twelve tribes of Israel into a nation, and the Mosaic law united them to God. As long as Israel kept the law, God would bless and protect them from the surrounding nations.

Elijah represents the prophets, the law's policemen. The prophets enforced the law, rebuking kings and urging wayward Jews to repent and return to the Lord Almighty.

As the First Testament closes, it doesn't only look backwards, it also looks ahead. God promises to "send the prophet Elijah to you before that great and dreadful day of the Lord comes" (v. 5). Jesus said this prophecy was fulfilled in John the Baptist, whose preaching of repentance prepared the way for His own ministry (see Matthew 17:10–13). John the Baptist is the new Elijah, and Jesus is the new Moses. Jesus delivers us from the bondage of sin, unites us into His body (the church), and gives us a new command—to "love one another" as He loves us (John 13:34).

Moses and Elijah seem to be the most important people of the First Testament. Their ultimate role is to point to Jesus, the most important person of both testaments and of everything. His life is the one that decisively counts. If we are in Jesus, then ours count too. We may be stuck now, but "our present sufferings are not worth comparing with the glory that will be revealed in us" (Romans 8:18).

Our present sufferings amount to a fraction of our unending life with Christ. The top number of a fraction may be large, but its real value shrinks as the bottom number increases (1/10 is greater than 1/100, which is greater than 1/1,000). What number would you assign to the situation you're stuck in? One thousand? One million? It may not matter what number you use. If the bottom number is infinity, the entire fraction approaches zero.

**Your pain is real, but it doesn't compare to the joy that will be yours forever in Jesus.**



The Mosaic law united Israel to God. How would remembering that Jesus is the new Moses encourage you to stay faithful to Him?

How well are you keeping Jesus' new command to "love one another" (John 13:34)?

# Day 30



Generations often don't understand each other. Older folks say youngsters are lazy and entitled. They fritter away their lives thumbing sarcastic texts on their handphones at chic coffee bars. Young people think the old fogies are whiners who refuse to retire, preventing the young from getting good jobs.

Does God have anything to say about this generational divide? Yes, He does. He ends His First Testament by promising that Elijah will come to "turn the hearts of the parents to their children, and the hearts of the children to their parents" (Malachi 4:6). Was that a surprise? Nothing in Malachi hinted at generational tension. Why bring it up at the end, seemingly from nowhere? Here's my guess: relationships are important, and they are always present, even when unspoken.

The good news of Jesus reconciles us to God and to each other. Jesus brings us together, starting with those who are closest to us. Godly parents and children won't harp on what bothers us about each other. Instead, we'll turn our hearts towards each other, focusing on what we share in Christ.

God does not make an empty promise. The angel told Zechariah, John the Baptist's father, that his son would "turn the hearts of the parents to their children" (Luke 1:17). This promise, however, is not a guarantee for everyone. The final words of the First Testament warn that if parents and children do not turn their hearts towards one another, which presumably comes from being reconciled with God, then God "will come and strike the land with total destruction" (Malachi 4:6).

He would follow through on this threat. Israel rejected John the Baptist and Jesus, so God did "strike the land with total destruction", using the Romans to raze Jerusalem to the ground in AD 70.

You and I can't control what others do, but we are responsible for our choices. We may be stuck in an apparently hopeless situation. It shows no sign of getting better. **We cannot change our circumstance, but we can change how we respond.** We can receive God's reconciliation in Christ, and leverage that to reconcile with others. At the end of your life, it won't matter where you were stuck, or for how long. The only thing that really matters is Jesus and the people He gave you to love. If that's what will matter then, why not get a head start? Love Jesus; love people.

**Think**Through

Consider God's
desire to reconcile
parents and children
with one another.
How is reconcilia-
tion with God and
others possible
(see 2 Corinthians
5:16–21)?

Whom do you need
to reconcile with?
What first steps can
you take right now?

# Going Deeper
# in Your Walk
# with Christ

Whether you're a new Christian or have been a Christian for a while, it's worth taking a journey through the Bible, book by book, to gain a deeper appreciation of who Jesus is and how we can follow Him.

Let faithful Bible teachers be your tour guides and help you draw closer to Christ as you spend time reading and reflecting on His Word.

**Journey**Through
## Job
*Christopher Ash*

**Journey**Through
## Hosea
*David Gibb*

**Journey**Through
## Amos
*J. R. Hudberg*

# Journey Through
# Joshua

If the book of Joshua were a movie, the Lord God would be the executive producer, director, screenwriter, and lead actor. For without the Lord God, nothing happens. Dig deeper into this historical narrative of the Israelites' conquering of the Promised Land under Joshua's leadership, and discover how you, too, can take courage and draw strength from God's abiding presence and wonderful promises to obey and serve Him wholeheartedly all the days of your life.

**David Sanford** loves God's Word and has served as the author, co-author, editor, managing editor, or executive editor for more than a dozen Bible and Bible-related projects. He and his wife, Renee Sanford, a noted author and editor in her own right, live in the Pacific Northwest region of the United States of America.

# Thirsting for more?

Check out **journeythrough.org**

...and many more available titles

**Explore other formats:**
- Read online
- Subscribe to a hard copy

# ABOUT THE PUBLISHER

Discovery House Publishing™
produces a wide array of premium
and quality resources that focus on Scripture,
show reverence for God and His Word,
demonstrate the relevance of vibrant faith,
and equip and encourage you to draw closer
to God in all seasons of your life.

**Discovery House**
P u b l i s h i n g™

# NOTE TO THE READER

We invite you to share your response to the message
of this book by writing to us at:

**5 Pereira Road #07-01
Asiawide Industrial Building
Singapore 368025**


or sending an email to:

**dhpsingapore@dhp.org**

www.ingramcontent.com/pod-product-compliance
Lightning Source LLC
Chambersburg PA
CBHW061254140726
47998CB00006B/2221